CONTEMPORARY STAINED GLASS
A Portfolio of Canadian Work

CONTEMPORARY

STAINED GLASS
A Portfolio of Canadian Work

Joel Russ and Lou Lynn

1985
DOUBLEDAY CANADA LIMITED, TORONTO, ONTARIO
DOUBLEDAY & COMPANY, INC., GARDEN CITY, NEW YORK

Library of Congress Catalog Card Number: 85-7029
Copyright ©1985 by Joel Russ and Lou Lynn
All rights reserved.

FIRST EDITION

Production by Paula Chabanais Productions
Designed by Catherine Wilson/Sunkisst Graphics
Typeset by Compeer Typographic Services Ltd.
Printed and bound in Hong Kong by Everbest Printing Co. Ltd.

Canadian Cataloguing in Publication Data
Russ, Joel, 1947–
   Contemporary stained glass

Includes index.
ISBN 0-385-23338-8

1. Glass painting and staining — Canada — 20th century.   I. Lynn, Lou 1950–   II. Title.

NK5313.R87 1985   748.5911   C85-098753-9

(Title page)
Pomp and Be Bop, 1982.
85 × 48 in. (215.9 × 121.9 cm)
Collection of the artist, Gundar
Robez. *Photograph by Joel Russ.*

CONTENTS

Preface

We have pursued a few main objectives in writing this book. The most obvious of these has been to present a cross-section of high-quality Canadian stained-glass work. It seemed unfortunate to us that few people were familiar with the work being done by this country's serious artists working in the stained-glass medium. In light of this concern, our role in researching and writing *Canadian Stained Glass* has been more curatorial than specifically critical. Neither of us is an art critic. We see the need for more evaluative discussions of the work of individual stained-glass artists, and of specific works within these artists' *oeuvres*, as well as the need for critically comparative discussions of the stained-glass work of various artists. First things first, however; it seemed to us paramount, at this time, simply to make the public more aware of the impressive nature of what is being done in stained glass in various regions of this country.

Along with our intent to present examples from the spectrum of contemporary stained-glass work done by Canadians, we have attempted to provide readers with the opportunity to gain insight into the minds of the artists: into their backgrounds and creative processes. Canada's stained-glass artists are at once members of a sort of fraternity as well as evident individuals. An active network exists among them, one with which many of the people whose work is represented in this book are involved. At the same time, these Canadian artists are aware, to varying degrees, of what is going on in stained glass in the rest of North America and on the international scene. Familiarity almost inevitably leads to influence—even if it's very subtle—on artistic attitudes and philosophy, if not on design. If Canada's serious stained-glass artists make up a community at all, however, it is a community of *individuals*. Individualism is intrinsic to what we in the modern period of the Western European cultural tradition understand as the nature of artistic vocation. Each of the artists included in this book works with a highly personal approach. Clearly, this is one reason why it is not often easy to look at a contemporary work in stained glass and understand fully why the artist designed it as he or she did. Naturally, then, our attempt to offer readers some insight into the artists' *oeuvres* and into individual works has required considerable cooperation from the artists themselves.

We had a third objective in mind as well at the beginning of this project. We wanted to discover if the Canadian glass scene, on the national level, had formed a foundation strong enough to support contemporary work of a caliber worthy of international respect. Further, if such work did exist in this country, we were interested in finding out whether or not its nature was distinguishable from the styles of contemporary European and American work. Personally, we feel that the work we've viewed in the course of our research has answered both these questions in the affirmative, but we leave it to readers who are knowledgeable in international contemporary stained glass to judge for themselves after viewing the works in *Contemporary Stained Glass: A Portfolio of Canadian Work*.

Selecting artists to be represented in a book such as this is always a difficult, even agonizing, task. There are many accomplished stained-glass artists now working in Canada, and various constraints prevented us from representing all of them in this book. While we regret this, we hope that ours will be but the first of many books to study the unfolding contemporary stained-glass scene in this country.

Joel Russ and Lou Lynn

Introduction

In the last two decades Canadian stained glass has come into its own. One stimulus prompting this efflorescence has been an influence from Europe, where a thousand-year tradition has recently been carried forward by an extensive and celebrated post-war revival in architectural stained glass. Beginning very gradually in the mid-sixties, some Canadians chose to study stained glass in Europe and bring what they learned back to Canada. During the same period, some European-born artists decided to immigrate to Canada. These dual conduits for European influences have primarily affected the realm of architectural stained glass — glass that is designed to be an integral functional and esthetic feature of a building.

The other major factor in this blossoming has been the tremendous increase of interest in the crafts — in things handmade. People involved with the craft renaissance that has manifested itself so visibly in North America have had considerable impact, on this continent, on both architectural stained glass and on a second, rather recently emerged medium for self-expression: the independent panel — a stained-glass work designed without an architectural setting in mind. We have reservations about calling any serious form of stained glass a "craft," even when its practitioners have come through the crafts movement. It can be said, however, that the influence that evolved out of the crafts scene has been a positive one, chiefly because in recent years virtually all the media usually regarded as crafts, whether the material be clay, wood, fiber, metal, or glass, have achieved a very high degree of sophistication and creativity at their upper levels. In each medium there are practitioners who have moved away from strict utility and clever commerciality and toward esthetic exploration and self-expression.

During the seventies, then, one stream of influence came over from Europe at a high level of actualization, while the contemporary North American development was rising to mingle with it. By now, it is not possible to separate clearly the influence of these two streams. On the one hand, there are Canadian artists now doing original work who credit the German, British, or French traditions as their chief influence or early inspiration; and, on the other hand, there are artists who see themselves as being directly influenced very little by anyone outside North America. However, through the energetic efforts of a number of Canadian artists, a network has developed among many of those most active in the Canadian stained-glass scene, resulting in an ongoing esthetic dialogue among these artists, whatever their background. Glass artists from Canada still sometimes go to Europe to study, and master glass artists from Europe come to Canada periodically to teach workshops in design; but the Canadian stained-glass scene has matured to the point where it largely functions on its own. There are now many Canadian artists working significantly in both major veins of stained glass: architectural glass and the independent panel.

It is not our intention to try to settle the large issue of what constitutes "art" and what "craft" — nor would it be possible. We have no doubt that the work shown in this book is of a caliber to justify the label "art"; nevertheless, in a certain sense of the term, the word "craft" is inescapable. Stained-glass windows or panels must be crafted — that is, made — just as a mural, an oil painting, or a sculpture must be crafted. In most cases, here in North America, the stained-glass artist is also his or her own artisan, designing and then making a piece in his or her own studio. But the design aspect and the craft aspect are reasonably separate tasks; either can be done well or poorly. Ignoring the craft aspect of the medium for the time being, we can say with confidence that there are Canadians designing in this medium who could work creditably — indeed, people who have done so — in painting, printmaking, or sculpture. Stained glass is simply the medium in which some artists have chosen to work, because they like it.

Perhaps it would be helpful to say something here about the origins of this art form, and then about Canada's stained-glass heritage.

The basic material of conventional stained glass is glass that, during its manufacture, has been colored by the addition of various metallic oxides. Archaeologists working in the Near East have uncovered objects made of diverse forms of colored glass dating from millennia before the Christian era. The Romans later developed a truly transparent glass. Rather surprisingly, some of the early Church fathers made references in their writings to colored windows in Christian basilicas, though of this glass no trace has as yet been found. But pieces of blue, green, amber, and red window glass dating back to a somewhat later period, the seventh century, have been found on the site of Monkwearmouth

Abbey in Sunderland, England. In some of the earliest-known examples of colored-glass windows, perforated sheets of marble, alabaster, wood, or some other material were built into the window openings of churches, with colored glass inserted into the perforations. Interestingly, the use of lead to hold the pieces of such a decorative window may date as far back as the fourth century A.D.

The Roman poet and satirist Horace (65–8 B.C.) mentioned in his writings that he decorated his room with pictures painted on glass, though it is unclear if these were colored; but it is very doubtful that these were much like the leaded panels with which we are familiar. While there is some documentary evidence to suggest the possible existence of *pictorial* leaded glass windows in Europe during the ninth century, a tenth-century history of the Church of Saint Remi in Rheims, France, states clearly that at the time of the history's writing, the church's windows depicted various scenes. The oldest example of a pictorial window to have been examined by modern authorities was a small panel possibly made in the ninth century; it was, tragically, destroyed in 1918.

During the thousand or more years in which stained glass as we know it has developed, it has undergone continual transformation with respect to design. Avoiding the simplistic observation that tastes change with the times, we can point to a number of factors contributing to the changing appearance of stained glass.

Technical developments relating to the materials and processes of the medium allowed and sometimes prompted artists to design in new ways. Because stained glass developed as an architectural art, changes in architecture have inevitably meant a changing role (and changes in design) for stained glass. This medium, like others, has through the centuries tended to develop in regional "schools," each with recognizable differences in technique and design; at the same time, artists of different schools have commonly been influenced and stimulated by what they have seen of each other's work. Noticeable parallels in stained glass to changing approaches to painting also suggest that stained-glass artists of centuries past paid attention not only to the work of other glass artists but also to the creations of artists who worked as fresco or easel painters. (Occasionally, too, the direction of influence has been reversed, as in the case of Rouault, whose paintings reflect an inspiration drawn from stained glass.) The stimuli behind the phases of stained-glass history are complex, and in retrospect the varied agents for change are more obvious in some instances than in others; even such a prosaic factor as a lack of certain raw materials has upon occasion considerably influenced technique and design.

The Gothic period of European art extended from the mid-twelfth century to the end of the fifteenth century. This is the epoch of the soaring cathedrals whose essential nature was made possible by a structural development: the ribbed vault. Gothic stained glass, especially the glass of the twelfth and thirteenth centuries, is regarded by most authorities as the high point in the history of architectural stained glass.

These authorities consider the integration of stained glass and architecture during these years to be unsurpassed, and the graphic approach of the hieratic design of these windows to be superlatively appropriate to the medium. According to this view, the Late Gothic's development of a more naturalistic depiction and of a tendency to force perspective into stained-glass design signaled an incipient decline in the level of architectural integration.

Europe's Renaissance began in the mid-fourteenth century; as it proceeded, art began to develop the esthetic of classicism, reflecting a Humanist view of life. Society's increasing secularization is reflected in the medium, as the portraits of window donors appear ever larger in the windows they donated, until they are the same size as the biblical figures depicted in the windows' scenes. From the standpoint of stained glass's role in architecture, a period lauded for the great technical advancements made in the art of painting is also commonly viewed as a period of esthetic decline in stained glass; as stained-glass artists increasingly emulated oil painters, they lost their own sense of purpose. From the late fifteenth century through most of the nineteenth century, stained glass was dominated by various forms of realist glass painting, with clear glass ultimately serving as a mere translucent canvas for painted-on designs and figures. Because such modes essentially ignored the unique and intrinsic qualities of the medium — the graphic potential of the leadline, and the light-modulating efficacy of specially made colored glass — the medium is seen as having been in conflict with itself during these centuries.

Stained glass originally came to the New World with the Church, one of the most pervasive and influential European institutions. Prior to the mid-nineteenth century, stained glass was imported to Canada from England and France to grace the walls of churches and other buildings. Early nineteenth-century glass in Canada thus exemplified the then-current styles of European enameled-glass design. It is possible that stained glass was designed and fabricated in Canada, using European-made glass, as early as the 1830s. At present, though, it is uncertain that stained glass was being designed and made in this country prior to the founding of Joseph McCausland's Toronto studio in 1857. This firm survives today as Robert McCausland Stained Glass Ltd. (Robert being Joseph's son), a studio that enjoys the distinction of being North America's oldest continuously operating stained-glass business. Numerous other stained-glass studios were founded, especially in Ontario, after McCausland's. Although churches constituted the mainstay market for stained glass, studios also made windows for university buildings, schools, and government buildings, as well as some windows—incorporating such things as landscapes and coats of arms—for private homes. Through the decades, Canadian firms still had to compete with European studios whose windows were imported. A number of English studios issued pattern catalogs and windows of the designs depicted could be ordered for any church, the production-line studios adapting the chosen pattern to fit. Ontario-based firms expanded their own market by sometimes shipping commissioned windows to other regions of the country. In 1870 windows were sent from Toronto to Fort Garry (now Winnipeg) by steamer, rail, and finally ox-cart; and, during the gold rush of 1898, some were delivered by dogsled to the Yukon and Northwest Territories.

In the latter part of the nineteenth century, while England was in the midst of the Gothic Revival in architecture, including rediscovery of the Gothic approach to stained glass, several of the prominent Ontario studios continued to design in styles, including the Pre-Raphaelite style, associated with earlier in the century — styles that were at that time considered passé in Europe. Toward the end of the century, both the approaches to design and the superior technique associated with Gothic Revival stained glass began to appear more consistently in the windows being made in Ontario. All through the nineteenth century and into the twentieth, the designers responsible for original Canadian glass designs were usually either immigrants from Europe or Canadian-born artists who went to Europe for training. But Canada followed England's lead, with the more productive stained-glass studios offering standardized designs as well as one-of-a-kind windows. These catalog designs often originated either in Britain or in the United States.

In Ontario the interest in stained glass broadened considerably during the 1880s and 1890s — a boom period for building. Stained glass was used extensively not only in churches and various public buildings, but also very frequently in both the stately homes of the well-to-do and the dwellings of the working class. Toronto still has a reputation for having more homes with stained glass and leaded clear glass in their windows than any other city in North America, and most of the homes so graced were built between 1880 and 1920. In Vancouver, stained glass made its appearance no later than the 1880s and proved popular enough that, by 1890, this very young city had a local studio, Henry Bloomfield and Sons. After World War I, however, interest in the decorative in architecture waned. Canadian enthusiasm for stained glass abated, and the form shrank back ever more toward its traditional ecclesiastical role. Some stained-glass firms were able to survive the Depression with a near-exclusive reliance on the church market.

Against the background of Victorian realism and pattern-book production that dominated the Canadian ecclesiastical glass of the time, one pioneer of modern glass established a new esthetic direction during the very difficult Depression years. Yvonne Williams set up her Toronto studio in 1930. Born in 1901, Williams had become interested in stained glass while an art student at the Ontario College of Art. After a series of visits to Europe, during which she studied the stained glass of the great cathedrals, she apprenticed at the Charles Connick Studios in Boston, before returning to Ontario. Williams took medieval styles of stained glass as the point of departure for her own original designs. During her more than fifty creative years, she designed some 150 windows for churches, chapels, and cathedrals. Williams also trained a number of important Canadian stained-glass artists, and her studio provided employment and technical facilities for skilled stained-glass designers like Stephen Taylor.

A few European glass artists came to Canada during the 1950s, but the market for stained glass was still very restricted—basically a church market. The diversified market stained glass now enjoys did not really come into being until the seventies. In the Toronto *Globe and Mail* in 1970, art commentator Kay Kritzwiser estimated that there were only about half a dozen professional stained-glass artists working in Ontario that year. The proliferation was soon to come, however.

In the past, Canadian stained glass tended to be derivative (and often eclectic), its influences coming from Europe. The first original American development of any consequence, the turn-of-the-century "opalescent art glass" pioneered by such artists as John LaFarge and Louis C. Tiffany, seems to have had rather little impact on Canadian stained-glass artists (except, perhaps, for a few in Quebec) until the North American crafts revival of the sixties and seventies. This revival saw a tremendous amount of interest in stained glass among American craftspeople and artists. Some very interesting new work from the western United States was publicized through a number of books written from the mid-seventies on, and this was an important spur to the development of the present Canadian glass scene. But during these same decades, design approaches were developing in Europe that were, once again, to have considerable impact on Canadian stained glass, though this time the European influence would stimulate rather than dominate.

In Europe since World War II, there has been a great deal of activity in the field of architectural stained glass. Cathedrals and churches, whether damaged during the war or merely fallen into disrepair, were rebuilt with contemporary stained glass. This led to expanded opportunities for stained glass in modern buildings, as well. The post-war, American Abstract Expressionists' rejection of everything traditional in painting inspired a similar rejection of stained glass's own lengthy traditions among German stained-glass artists, and the resulting innovation was remarkably successful in both graphic design and architectural integration. In designing for modern structures, these artists have been able to work closely with architects from the very inception of a building, and this has made the integration of the glass and the building all the more thorough. Many North American artists view such post-war German glass designers as Ludwig Schaffrath, Johannes Schreiter, Jochem Poensgen, and others as pre-eminent in contemporary architectural-glass design. The importance of the German artists' influence on one stage or another of many Canadian artists' development should be evident to anyone reading the profiles in this book.

More than any previous generation, today's glass artists have ready access to a tremendous range of international art history. A design may as easily be sparked by Tutankhamen's coffin mask as by some aspect of the work of a stained-glass designer of the past or present. However, inspiration and direction are just as likely to come from some source outside art altogether: flying through the clouds in a light aircraft, for instance; or watching the changing light on the eastern coastline of Nova Scotia. The field is virtually wide open. There is probably more widespread originality in Canadian stained glass design now than ever before.

What is involved in the designing of stained glass? A long answer to the question is contained in the many statements and viewpoints of the artists profiled in this book. But we can say a bit on this subject at the outset. With respect to the graphic aspect of stained glass, the artist may work with line, point, shape, spatial relationships, color, tonality, and possibly even perspective, in a manner similar to a painter or printmaker. In the case of glass built into a building, the graphic aspect should in most instances relate in some way to the architecture, either by referring directly to the architecture, as an extension or elaboration of the architect's design, or by taking a judiciously determined counterpoise role to the elements of that design. In such a case, the considerations of the stained-glass artist might be similar to those of a muralist.

There are crucial differences between stained glass and painting or printmaking, however, because, for one thing, virtually all the types of glass used in stained-glass art transmit light. Those special characteristics that set the stained-glass medium apart from other media (like painting and printmaking) necessitate a set of artistic considerations that are peculiar to the medium. We'll confine our discussion, for the moment, to architectural stained glass.

A stained-glass window is illumined when "white" light from the sun or some other source passes through it, giving it the radiant quality that we associate with stained glass viewed from inside a church during daylight hours. But at the same time, scenes and objects on the opposite side of a stained-glass window are also potentially visible to the viewer. The designer must decide just *how* visible these external scenes or objects should be — decide, that is, whether to use glass that is transparent, glass that is just translucent, or some of each. Sometimes artists go beyond a simple consideration of how much of what is beyond the window should remain visible; they may decide to use specific types of glass in a window because their refractive qualities will incorporate and *alter*, in specific ways, the visual environment that lies beyond the window.

The fact that a stained-glass window admits light into a building results in another important distinction between the concerns of the painter and those of the architectural-glass artist. The painter is concerned with reflected light, the stained-glass artist with transmitted light. When daylight, particularly direct sunlight, passes through a stained-glass window, it has an effect both on the room's appearance and on its general feeling or atmosphere. If an interior's only source of natural light is a stained-glass window, the room's atmosphere can be very strongly influenced by the stained glass. Not only will a person notice the compositional, or graphic, quality of the window when looking directly at it, but he or she will be aware, though perhaps only subliminally, of the degree of the room's illumination, the coloration of the room's light, and the presence of colored shapes or spectral effects projected onto the floors and walls when direct sunlight passes through the window. As well, the fact that the quality of illumination changes during the hours of the day and during the seasons of the year makes the design task facing the artist all the more complex.

There is at least one other major difference between painting and stained-glass design. The stained-glass artist, whether designing architectural glass or an independent panel, is working with a medium whose basic materials are inherently hard to work with. Leaving aside the question of what constitutes good or poor results in either medium, it is mechanically much easier to push paint around on a canvas or other surface with a brush than it is to cut myriad odd-shaped pieces of glass, fit them properly to one another, and fix them in place with lead cames (H-channel strips) or copper foil and lead-tin solder. At atmospheric temperatures, glass is a brittle, fragile, unforgiving substance. It is tricky to handle, and the stained-glass designer can never forget this. Anyone who has ever tried to shape some of this unsympathetic stuff with a glass cutter will immediately recognize the technical prowess and design ingenuity of those whose work is illustrated here. Many effects that can be obtained by the painter working in oils cannot be obtained in stained glass, even when the glass pieces are painted using the traditional enameling technique. In any medium, the artist succeeds only when he or she accepts the nature of that medium, complete with its limitations and difficulties as well as its potential advantages. As with any art form, in the hands of an accomplished designer and skilled artisan, stained glass exhibits its special strengths in dimensions that the products of other media cannot enter.

Such stained-glass works as windows and room-dividing screens that are built into architectural structures are classified as architectural stained glass and, as such, are consistent with stained glass's historically honored functions. The other major vein of stained glass consists of works that are not built into a structure but rather are designed to be contemplated as isolated esthetic objects, just as paintings, sculptures, and fine photographs are. These are the independent panels, alternatively referred to as "autonomous" or "exhibition" panels. The contemporary independent panel has historical antecedents — the heraldic panels of the late Middle Ages and after are an example — but in fact this form has only recently become bold enough to seek recognition as a medium for serious self-expression and esthetic exploration in its own right.

Widespread recognition of the independent panel as a fine-art form is not easily obtained. Stained-glass artist Robert Jekyll emphasized to us one of the obstacles: because it requires backlighting, the panel has suffered from being difficult to display in most art galleries. This handicap, which has effectively deprived the medium of the serious attention of gallery directors and, thus, of public notice, has certainly done nothing to further its acceptance as a legitimate art form. However, the situation could well change in the future. Exciting plans are currently unfolding for the construction, in Waterloo, Ontario, of North America's first gallery especially designed to display stained glass.

This development is indicative of the blossoming that has recently occurred in Canadian stained glass. Not so long ago, Ontario supported only a handful of stained-glass artists. During the sixties and early seventies, it was very difficult for a Canadian to get much training, in Canada, in either the artistic or technical side of stained glass. In 1970, if a Canadian wanted real stimulation or instruction in the design aspect of stained glass, he or she had to go to Europe. This was, of course, what Canadian-born designers had been doing since the nineteenth century. In Europe one could study both the magnificent work found in the great cathedrals and the often excellent examples tucked away in little country chapels. There were the artists who were developing (not only for churches but also for secular public buildings) the new vocabularies that characterize any living art form. And there, too, were the schools and apprenticeship programs — the opportunities to study with master stained-glass artists — needed by any serious student. We are fortunate that some Canadians have chosen to study in Europe; for this, combined with the fact that European glass designers have immigrated to this country, has encouraged Canadian glass artists, continually, to measure their work against the highest standards.

It is now far more possible to acquire a good grounding in the stained-glass medium without leaving Canada than it was even a decade ago. The basic techniques — glass-cutting, leading, copper-foiling, and soldering — can be learned through a beginner's course in nearly any sizable city in Canada (and in many smaller communities). Virtually all of the larger population centers have courses — offered through commercial glass studios, colleges, night-school programs, and so on — that teach intermediate and advanced techniques. Books on technique are no longer difficult to obtain. Books on historical and contemporary stained glass in the United States, Germany, England, and other countries are now reasonably available in Canada, and many libraries have them. In the United States, several stained-glass journals are currently published — some long-established, some new — that treat technical, esthetic, and marketing matters; there are also a number of European journals. All of these are quite popular with Canadian glass artists. Organizations like Artists in Stained Glass, Atlantic Glass Artisans, and l'Association Québécoise des Verriers help to keep the stained-glass network alive among both professionals and serious amateurs. These organizations serve at least two very essential roles: they organize design workshops taught by master stained-glass artists, from Europe and the United States, as well as from Canada; and they mount exhibitions of interesting Canadian work for both the public and other artists to view.

All this is certainly not to say that there is no longer a good reason for a Canadian interested in stained glass to leave Canada to study elsewhere. Opportunities for genuine studio apprenticeship in stained glass are still extremely limited here, and Europe and the United States have more in the way of ongoing institutional programs for training. Furthermore, Europe is home to the great cathedrals as well as to much of the best modern architectural stained glass, and there is no substitute for studying stained glass in its architectural context. As suggested earlier, however, Canada is seeing the development of a vital and complex stained-glass scene of its own, and some interesting work is now being done by artists who have never studied abroad.

The first thing readers may notice in this book is the remarkable divergence of the design approaches of the various artists represented. Art, when it is not purely derivative or mannered, is as varied as the artists who make it. And why, in our modern era, shouldn't we enjoy this situation? One stands, perhaps, to be as much enriched by this variety as by the strength or beauty of remarkable individual works.

It is essential to remember that architectural designs are specifically related to functions and settings, representing the disciplined response of a particular artist to a specific set of circumstances. Canada is a diverse nation—geographically, historically, economically, and culturally—and this is reflected in the variegated architecture that has developed here over several centuries. Because of the relationship of architectural art to architecture, the designs of artists who work in architectural glass reflect the country's architectural variety. As well, stained-glass artists demonstrate a range of different attitudes to the question of exactly what the proper role of architectural glass is—partly because they have received their training in different ways and places, and partly because they have been differently influenced by the work and theories of various artists before them. Personal factors always affect the work, even when that work is an example of large-scale architectural glass in a public building.

Autonomous work is an open field for the imagination of the artist, and personal reasons for the diversity of design come very much into play. What interests different artists in terms of stained glass's potential always varies tremendously; but this fact is underscored when the work in question is independent of architecture. Also, there can be no doubt that each artist has his or her own special strengths as a designer; and, of course, different artists have varying degrees of interest in and ability with the technical aspects of the medium.

Diversity has been an essential characteristic of twentieth-century art. As in other media, the different approaches taken by various stained-glass artists are sources of endless debate, cavil, and controversy. This seems inevitable, and the net result of this dialogue is no doubt a healthy one. We can only say that the diversity in the stained glass that we have seen in various parts of Canada has made the subject all the more fascinating for us; we feel that this country's stained-glass scene is the more vital for it.

Marcelle Ferron

As Marcelle Ferron talked to us about her life as an artist and her career in stained glass, her mood ranged from intense animation to quiet reminiscence. A petite woman with a gentle face and sparklingly intelligent eyes, she projects a passion not only for her work but, it seems, for life in general. During our interview, she strove intently to communicate her thoughts to us in English — the language of recourse — and we struggled from time to time to propose a word or phrase that seemed to be eluding her.

"I began as a painter," Madame Ferron told us. "After that I did sculpture. I wanted to be an architect, when I was

LA PRESSE

J.R.

young. But at that time it was impossible for a woman to be an architect — she would be at the bottom of the scale." Then, with reference to the environmental and public nature of her stained-glass work, she added, "Later I came back to architecture, perhaps to its social relation with people." For Marcelle Ferron, art is for the people.

Born in 1924, in Louiseville, Quebec, to a family of means, Marcelle Ferron became interested in art during her mid-teens through the influence of an art teacher at the convent school she attended. Although her mother painted, she died when Marcelle was young. But Monsieur Ferron, a man with socially progressive ideas, was quite supportive of his childrens' desire to pursue careers related to the arts: Marcelle's brother Jacques, and her sister, Madeleine, became writers well known in Quebec; her brother Paul is a noted art collector. Ferron studied for a year (1942–43) at l'École des Beaux Arts in Montreal, under Jean-Paul Lemieux and Simone Hudon.

Beginning in 1945, Ferron spent several years under the tutelage of Paul-Émile Borduas, the firebrand leader of *les Automatistes* and one of the most important Canadian painters of the twentieth century. The *Automatistes* group pursued a fresh, abstract approach to painting, seeking to unchain artistic spontaneity from the fetters of conventional esthetic considerations. At that time, in Quebec, such artistic presumption was necessarily of considerable social — even moral — significance. The oppressive weight of tradition on Quebec society, and consequently on its art, compelled Borduas to publish his *Refus Global* ("Complete Rejection") manifesto in 1948 — a statement that caused such a stir that Borduas lost his teaching position at l'École de Meuble. (Ferron was among the fifteen of Borduas's students and supporters who signed this document.) Borduas ultimately resigned himself

PLATE 1: (Opposite) Champ de Mars Métro station, 1968. Total area approx. 2000 sq. ft. (185.8 sq. m) Montreal, Quebec.

to an expatriate's life, moving from Quebec to New York, and later to Paris, where he died in 1960.

In the 1940s, then, Ferron was one of the new generation of abstract painters. She showed her paintings, done in the amiably vigorous style associated with *les Automatistes*, at her first solo exhibition, in Montreal in 1949. She had her first exhibition of sculpture and drawings in 1952, shortly before she left Canada to live and pursue art in Europe for nearly thirteen years. During those years she returned to Montreal only periodically and for short visits. Ferron mostly painted during her first few years abroad, but later studied printmaking with Stanley Hayter in Paris. After a time she acquired a house and garden near Montparnasse. During these years abroad, Ferron showed her artwork in a continual succession of solo and group exhibitions in Europe, Canada, and the United States.

From 1963 to 1965, Ferron worked in the Paris stained-glass studio of Michel Blum. She soon came to love stained glass and learned all the conventional techniques for working with it; but she ultimately grew to dislike the pyramidal hierarchy within which stained-glass designers and fabricators worked in France at that time. When Ferron returned to Quebec in the mid-1960s — this time to stay — she was competent to undertake commissions in stained glass. She knew that it would be easier to begin such a career in Canada than in France.

Madame Ferron believes that there is no substitute for the artisan's experience of the medium, and that technical understanding, though insufficient in itself, is essential to artistic success in stained glass. In her own work there was, from the start, an inescapable influence from her painting on her stained glass. "You cannot have twenty years of experience in painting with big forms without that influencing the glass," Madame Ferron declares. "But you must think with the material, and that takes a long time to learn. You must get used to the light where you work. I made mistakes in my first window when I arrived back from France, where the light was very subtle. The snow during the winter here was too intense. It made the colors in my window look feeble." Madame Ferron learned the essential lessons by dedication to her new medium, taking the inevitable risks. There was, in fact, a seven-year period in her career during which she did not paint but designed stained glass instead.

All of Madame Ferron's stained-glass works are executed using Saint-Just "antique" glass, which offers her roughly three thousand shades from which to choose. That Ferron relishes this opportunity to select carefully just the shade she wants reflects an aspect of her life philosophy. "It is impossible for me to think in black and white," she told us at one point. "What concern me are the nuances." However, this does not in any way imply that Ferron is timid about strong color. She is not — as can be seen in the accompanying plates.

The Champ de Mars Métro station in Montreal (*See* Plate 1), which Madame Ferron was commissioned to do in 1968, represents a consummate secular stained-glass environment. Three of its exterior walls are composed of architectural glass, the expanses measuring thirty, forty, and sixty feet wide. Overall, these windows are approximately half clear glass. Resilient, levitating colored forms and bands of color move freely through this colorless space. The reader will notice that these colored areas alternate in functioning as negative and positive space in the design of the windows. An interesting sense of balance has been achieved, yet there is nothing labored here. The sense of movement in these windows is pronounced, and this, combined with the striking contrast between the clear glass and the colored shapes, creates quite a spectacular

PLATE 2: Third-floor courthouse windows, 1982. Total area approx. 2800 sq. ft. (260.12 sq. m) Granby, Quebec.

effect for anyone lingering in or walking through the station. Again, the appropriateness of the large shapes is apparent. As it is, this stained-glass environment is delightful and invigorating; were the shapes more minute, fragmented, or profuse, the environment might easily be agitating, instead.

In discussing her approach to design, Madame Ferron says, "I don't care if people look at my large, colorful, dancing forms and say that I am naive. I prefer to be naive."

It is a forthright and charming remark, although the work of such an obviously cultivated woman could scarcely be called naive. After all, not only has Ferron lived and traveled extensively in Europe, she has also sojourned in the Orient and Indonesia. Her works have been shown at the Grand Palais and the Louvre in Paris, the Tate Gallery in London, and the Osaka Exhibition in Japan; and they are part of the permanent collections of the National Gallery of Canada, the Musée du Québec, and the Musée Stedelijk in Amsterdam. Yet the childlike spontaneity is there, and for Madame Ferron it is sustained by a philosophical insight.

"Artists are very naive," she observes. "Their role is to bring color. When civilizations are tired, they take out the color. So for me it was very important to bring color to buildings, to make a dynamism in buildings in a country where there is white — no flowers — for six months of the year."

As we talked with her, it became evident that Madame Ferron's tastes in painting have always run toward the spontaneous and colorful. She mentions Matisse as a long-time favorite. Her tastes in stained glass also run toward the colorful. Still, it is rather surprising to hear what type of

MARCELLE FERRON 23

stained-glass work she feels has influenced her most: "It is very conservative to say, but I think the biggest influence was the big cathedrals in Europe. I saw Chartres more than forty times. You could not separate the architecture from the stained glass there."

If there is any connection between examples so disparate in approach as Ferron's work and that in Chartres, it must be in the purposeful integration of glass into both the form and social function of a specific architectural site — in the attempt to achieve a particular influence on the light in an expansive human environment.

The courthouse in Granby, Quebec, was designed with the extensive use of stained glass in mind. Most of the south-facing wall in the main part of this stately, modern, three-story edifice is made up of glass designed by Marcelle Ferron. This wall of stained glass is a very impressive external feature of the building during the day. The glass work on each of the three floors of the courthouse (*See* Plates 2 and 3) fits into a comprehensive scheme: the same basic gestures — the arc, the ellipse, and the ribbon-like band—are used in the design of each long expanse of window. The color is bold. There is a strong similarity between the over-all design of these windows and that of the windows in the Champ de Mars Métro station, though here transparent colored glass of moderate saturation has been used as the background in place of clear glass.

There is nothing dreary about the Granby courthouse. Its interior is filled with warm light. Its windows dance and sing. While incorporating the straight line and the angle, which lead the eye and bring a reference to the architecture into play, the windows' curvilinear shapes offer a lively contrast to the angular lines of the building's interior. There can be no doubt that the building would be much the poorer without its stained glass.

For Marcelle Ferron, stained-glass design can never be simply a matter of integrating a graphic design into an architectural configuration. The glass must relate also to the building's whereabouts and function, and to the quality of light and the seasonal changes that will be part of its environment. The glass must be meaningful within the cultural setting, as well. This range of considerations must, in a sense, become part of the artist as the design is contemplated. Only then can a design be produced that will communicate in the desired way with the people who will use the building. "I have a commission to do a stained-glass wall in Tokyo," Madame Ferron says. "You cannot do in Japan what you do in the courthouse in Granby — because of the light, because of the architecture, because of the culture. You must feel the place, feel the culture."

At the time we interviewed her, Madame Ferron had already visited Japan and appraised the situation for which she would design this glass. She feels that the time she has spent in Japan and her exposure to its culture and its art have led to some subtle differences in her approach to work she has done here in Canada. "There is an evident influence on my work. Perhaps now it is more simplified, perhaps less noisy. But perhaps it is losing something, too, from a certain point of view."

It will be no surprise to those who are aware of Marcelle Ferron's career as a painter that painting is still very important to her. It is a prime field of experimentation for her. There is an immediacy of result possible in that medium that can, of course, never be obtained in the technically complicated medium of stained glass. There is also the aspect of liberty: "Painting is a very, very private laboratory," the artist comments. "You are responsible to yourself. If you are upset by problems, at that moment your paintings are not good. Painting is a mirror. But in architectural work you are constrained by givens. You must use your accumulated wisdom of life." But this does not mean that the work in one

PLATE 3: Outside view of courthouse windows, 1982. Total area approx. 2800 sq. ft. (260.12 sq. m) Granby, Quebec.

J.R.

medium does not nurture the other. For example, the arcing shapes the artist sometimes uses in her paintings are also evident in her glass designs.

Madame Ferron expresses keen interest in what the younger generation of Canadian stained-glass artists are doing. Although she feels that the training available in Canada is generally not as thorough or deep as that available in Europe, she has praise for the conceptual openness and opportunity for newcomers in the current Canadian stained-glass scene. She is enthusiastic about the technical experimentation being carried out by so many artists working in glass, expecting that it will result in some interesting new paths in self-expression.

Madame Ferron taught in the School of Architecture at Laval University from 1967–70, and in Laval's School of Visual Arts from 1970–79. Consequently, she is accustomed to have young people come to her to discuss the challenges of working in various media, including stained glass. "When you have become a certain age, things change. You have become known — and it's not your fault, it just snowballs. You become a professor. Young artists come to you to talk and exchange ideas about stained glass. But I try to discard the professorial attitude, to arrive at another kind of exchange." For Madame Ferron the exchange must be free, lively, creative, and, yes, mutual.

Movement. Growth. Life. These are the things with which an artist deals. The artist notices, feels, incorporates. "I work every day," Madame Ferron says. "But the artist can be listening to music, or even traveling, and he is still working. I think the artist is privileged, because he loves his work, and it is his life."

David Wilde

I want to stay away from making just another beautiful window. When I design a window, I want it to be something that can be intellectually appreciated, rather than just a collection of straight lines and colors."

Given the purely decorative nature of so much of what has been produced in stained glass in the last century, this is a provocative statement. It is all the more intriguing when it comes from someone as usually relaxed and waggish as David Wilde.

Wilde takes his stained-glass work completely seriously and is meticulous in his approach. Focused on architectural work, he is accustomed to making a comprehensive assessment of the requirements of a given situation before beginning to

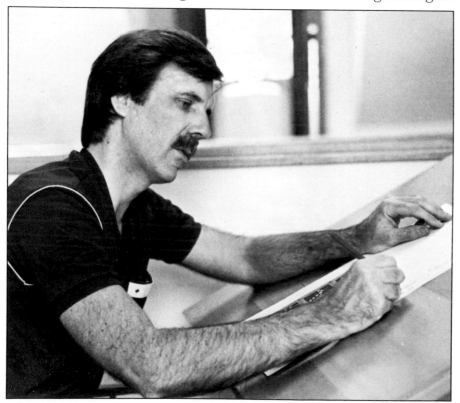

design. There are essential considerations besides the ones involved with a strict graphic integration of the glass design with the architecture. In Wilde's view, "The artist must be sensitive to lines of sight, to whether the client wants privacy or wants a lot of light, to the directional orientation of the building and the window openings, to what the light is going to be like at different times of the year, to whether the window's pattern will project against a wall (and what kind of wallpaper may be on that wall), to what the floor-covering in that place is. All these things go through your mind when you're in the building, and it's hard to sort it all out at first. But after a while, you don't even have to write it down — it becomes automatic." Nevertheless, he adds, if a window does not succeed at the graphic level, and if it does not complement the building into which it is set, these more subtle considerations are all for naught.

The three-panel window in the foyer of Toronto's Koffler Gallery (*See* Plate 4) was designed for a completely finished setting. It is a good example of Wilde's graphic style and a successfully integrated piece of architectural work. The Koffler Gallery, located in Toronto's Jewish Community Centre, hosted an exhibition of stained glass in the spring of 1984, and Wilde designed the window for this occasion. The suggested theme of the exhibition was the Passover. Wilde's window was designed in loose interpretation of the theme of deliverance, using the rainbow as the primary symbol. At the symbolic level, the panel "reads" from right to left. "The random colors on the far right grid suggest a lack of order — confusion," Wilde explains. "Then there is the doubly offset center grid, with its seven large squares, representing the seven tribes, and the orange arrangement, which I meant to represent the burning bush, giving order as we move across. On

PLATE 4: *Untitled Grid Trilogy*, Koffler Gallery, 1984. 11 × 3 ft. (3.35 × .91 m) Toronto, Ontario.

the left is a green grid, suggesting cultivated land, settlements: the Promised Land.''

The piece presents a contrast of regularities that somehow makes the formal look informal. Near the lower edge of the window runs a broad horizontal band composed of an orderly spectrum of six primary and secondary colors, from red to violet, bordered by slightly wider ribbons of a very dark green. Since most of the design's upper portion is higher-key and lighter in visual mass, the rainbow band functions to give weight to the window's bottom, anchoring the design in the setting. There is a strong grid pattern in white, semi-opaque glass running behind this broad band, serving to tie the design's upper portion together and to soften the effect of the window. The checkerboard-like grids at the right and left ends are oriented on a slant, and these are balanced by the middle section, of a similar pattern, oriented on a slant in the opposite direction. This middle section is enclosed within a narrow red band that forms a triangular border, one of the design's strong elements. The red here and in the rainbow band relates to the red of the cushions on the bench below the window.

With its extensive inclusion of clear glass, the window permits the entry of a substantial amount of light; yet its design is dense enough to hold the eye at the window's plane, making it a strong feature in the gallery foyer. The window's bias-oriented elements and variety of colors add a little piquancy to the otherwise smooth regularity of the foyer area. The over-all effect of the work is fresh and impressive.

"I come by what I do on my own," Wilde says. "I don't have any preconceived notions of what is contemporary. I like straight lines, and I like color, whether people these days say that's where it's at or not." Wilde makes extensive use, in his designs, of strong color, straight lines, borders, geometry, diagonal alignment of compositional elements, and asymmetry. The careful use of these ingredients gives much of his work a feeling of ordered vitality and cheerfulness. Though Wilde's windows may have an intellectual dimension to them, they are in no way arid.

A principle that is certainly important to Wilde's work is definition. He favors the traditional leaded technique because of the separation it affords to areas of color. He also likes the emphasis that can be given to colors by their careful placement in relation to one another. "I like the stark contrast in the pieces I've been doing lately. A yellow is really *yellow* when you have it beside black and white. I think [glass sculptor] Karl Schantz has been an influence—his work with Vitrolite laminated in a rainbow of colors, surrounded by black bars of glass."

At the time we interviewed him, Wilde had for a number of years been deeply involved in the Toronto art-glass community. He was then the current (and very dedicated) president of Artists in Stained Glass, the Toronto-based group that has been the most successful of Canada's associations of serious stained-glass artists. He shared a large studio space with Robert Jekyll, glass-sculptor Schantz, and Gundar Robez for a period of time. Artistic stimulation and exchange of ideas have never been a problem for him.

Wilde originally became interested in the medium when he began to collect old stained-glass panels that were turning up at garage sales. Eventually, he began to try an amateur's hand at repairing stained glass and at making small pieces. Later, he signed up for a course given by Robert Jekyll at Georgian College in Barrie, Ontario (in June 1978). It was at this point that he realized that "there was more to stained glass than birdies, sailboats, and repairing old windows." Wilde's involvement soon became quite deep. He began to collect what became an impressive library of books on stained glass that he now counts as a real aid in the evolution of his understanding of the medium. Besides attending many of the professional conferences held in eastern Canada and the eastern United States, Wilde has participated in a number of design seminars, including those in Toronto led by Jochem Poensgen (1983) and Johannes Schreiter (1984). In 1984, as well, he made a brief but carefully planned visit to Ireland for the purpose of getting a firsthand look at Irish stained glass and meeting some Irish stained-glass artists.

Though Wilde's interest is primarily in stained glass's architectural role, he has done — and has bought — some autonomous panels. "The independent panel is important to me because I've moved a number of times, and I would not want to leave a work of art behind." This is an interesting insight into the genuine need for portable art in a society where people typically change residences every few years. "But," he adds, "the independent panel is non-site-specific." Factors such as lighting and the general surroundings in the situations in which panels may be placed cannot be controlled by the artist once the piece has been sold, so the effectiveness of the panel may be in jeopardy.

But whether architectural or independent, all of Wilde's stained-glass designs are non-representational. "I don't like seeing anything I can identify at all in stained glass," he admits. He expresses an acute disdain for the mediocre figurative work that was to be found commonly in the commercial stained glass of the 1970s. Though not a uniformly held view, this dislike of pictorial design is common among contemporary Canadian stained-glass artists and contrasts with the attitudes of their American counterparts. Wilde attributes this feature of the Canadian scene to the strong influence of modern German and English stained glass on Canada's serious designers.

Wilde finds sources of design inspiration in a very broad range of experience: in graphics or photographs in magazines; in TV shows and commercials; in almost anything visual. Since he has no personal interest in representational work, it is not images themselves he studies but visual patterns that may initiate an esthetic odyssey in his own imagination.

The idea for Wilde's independent panel *Telecommunication* (*See* Plate 5) was sparked by a Bell Canada TV commercial depicting electrons flashing across a grid. In the panel Wilde makes conspicuous use of the principle of rhythm in both foreground and background. The configuration of the light-blue bands against the stable substantiality of the background verticals creates a sense of movement. The whole design is enlivened by numerous randomly placed accent elements, such as the glass jewels in the foreground bands. The design is interesting for its effectiveness despite the use of background and foreground patterns of roughly equal definition and visual intensity.

While David Wilde seems a little more insistent than some artists in his attitude toward representational work, his feel-

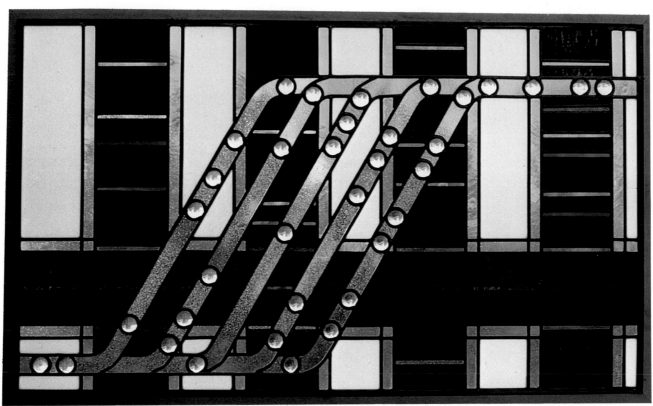

D.W.

PLATE 5: *Telecommunication*,
1984. 50 × 30 in. (127 × 76.2 cm)
Collection of artist.

ings are based on thoughtful reflection about what the term "stained glass" has come to mean in the minds of many Canadians. "I've personally seen a church window design, on a particular biblical theme, repeated six times, with only the slightest changes to fit into the different size and shape window openings in various churches — all of these having been done over fifty years in the life of one studio. I don't want *that* to be our stained-glass heritage. Let's do something that's personal, more original. I don't look at representational art as being as serious for today's sensibilities as non-representational art is."

Wilde is equally adamant that serious glass artists in Canada are, indeed, playing a role in the contemporary development of the art. "We Canadians have an identity of our own in stained glass. We're an essential part of the North American stained-glass scene, and recognized as such. And that is a thrill."

Robert Jekyll

W hat is a 'professional' artist? Unless you go through the *struggle* of being an artist—with all the privations, the limitations, and all the stuff that goes along with it — your work doesn't suffice. There's something missing: the compelling urge to express yourself in certain ways, the continuous re-education."

The struggle of which Robert Jekyll speaks is one that he himself embraced years ago. In 1971 he was an aeronautical engineer in the Maritime Command (formerly the Royal Canadian Navy) of the Canadian Armed Forces, living in Montreal. He was also a weekend painter. That year, he and some friends who were also serious amateurs planned an exhibition on the theme of "painting related to other media," and it fell on Jekyll to explore the then rather neglected medium of stained glass. The need for materials took him to some commercial studios in Montreal and Toronto. The search for technical information led him to English designer Patrick Reyntiens's book, *The Technique of Stained Glass*. Jekyll did indeed produce his stained-glass panel, and displayed it along with other works in this exhibition.

This was a pivotal period in Jekyll's life, for he had been contemplating leaving the Navy and pursuing some new but as yet undetermined career. The search for this "something new" took him to Europe in the summer of 1972. As a result of his recently piqued interest in stained glass, he made a point of meeting Patrick Reyntiens, in England, at the beginning of his journey. He learned that Reyntiens was then organizing a course, for the fall of that year, at Burleighfield House school, in Loudwater, Buckinghamshire. After talking with Jekyll about his life up to that point and the interest he had recently developed in stained glass, Reyntiens decided to accept him into the one space still open in the course.

Jekyll commenced study at Burleighfield House upon returning from his summer travels.

Jekyll's previous formal art training consisted of painting instruction he had received as a boy. He feels that Reyntiens made a good teacher for him partly because he too was a painter and well understood the problem of capturing in stained glass something of the freshness and immediacy one takes for granted in painting. During his second year of working with Reyntiens, Jekyll served as the master's studio manager, taking on considerable responsibility for some big commissions. The time Jekyll spent with Reyntiens thus fostered both his artistic and his practical confidence with the medium.

While abroad, Jekyll made a point of studying at firsthand the stained glass of different periods, in various parts of Europe. An important part of this study was the investigation of contemporary German architectural glass. Looking back on the whole of his European experience, Jekyll comments, "If you are going to see examples of stained glass that are important, that represent developments throughout history, you have to go abroad. You don't find these examples in Canada. My recommendation to anybody who's serious is, 'Get yourself to Europe.'"

When Jekyll returned to Canada in 1974, he brought with him a supply of then hard-to-get stained-glass supplies and a resolve to set up a studio in Toronto. He relished the challenge of being a part of the process of revitalizing a tradition-bound art form. Jekyll established his career in stained-glass design at a time when the medium had not as yet been rediscovered on the popular level in North America.

Still, there were by this time a few other new-generation stained-glass artists in Toronto, who would sometimes gather for an evening of shoptalk in one or another of their studios. In December of 1975, this growing circle held a meeting to discuss what they felt to be a lamentable situation: the clerestory windows of the Canadian parliament's Senate Chamber in Ottawa were to be designed by a federal government employee without any open approach to the community of Canadian stained-glass artists — as had previously happened with respect to the windows for the House of Commons Chamber. Jekyll and the others drafted a petition to protest what they saw as an unfairly circumscribed procedure.

PLATE 6: (Top) Hodge residence, 1983. 36 × 18 in. (91.4 × 45.7 m) Toronto, Ontario.

PLATE 7: (Bottom) Wigle residence, 1984. 30 × 72 in. (76.2 × 182.9 cm) Toronto, Ontario.

Out of this ad hoc solidarity grew what was to become Canada's largest organization for stained-glass practitioners, Artists in Stained Glass (AISG). AISG holds regular general meetings of its membership, mounts public exhibitions, presents public lectures, slide talks, and films, and has organized a Master Stained-Glass Workshop series through which it offers classes with world-famous glass designers. Through the years, AISG's mandate has been a broad one: to promote the development of contemporary stained glass in Canada. Robert Jekyll served as the organization's president from 1976–81 and edited its magazine, *The Leadline*, from 1976–82.

Alongside his devoted work for and with the organization, Jekyll waged the struggle of the serious artist — the diligence that accompanies esthetic development and the effort of learning to meet the requirements of the marketplace. He has produced a sizable body of work over the years, much of which consists of residential windows.

An interesting example of Jekyll's residential work is the window ensconced in weaver Bill Hodge's renovated Victorian house (*See* Plate 6). The house has a vintage Victorian stained-glass transom above the living-room window. Jekyll wanted to do something that related to the existing Victorian window but that also had a very strongly modern look. The circle in the center of Jekyll's window relates to the circular motif in the Victorian window, and the color scheme and use of a border relate to the older window, as well. "It was my first excursion into what I would call 'broken geometry,' " Jekyll comments. "One of the problems with Victorian windows was that they were very rigid in their geometry. This window is a bit of a commentary on the Victorian penchant for formalized shapes."

There is a merriment to Jekyll's window, an almost carnivalesque quality created by the brightly colored striped areas bursting through. The contrast between the background order and this exuberant eruption is perhaps like that between ordinary days and festive days.

The window in the living room of the Wigle residence (*See* Plate 7) uses a similar compositional approach in a more low-key treatment. For this window, in the home of an art consultant and her physician husband, says Jekyll, "I was given *carte blanche*. The Hodge window was the point of departure for this one, which is vertically rather than horizontally oriented." Jekyll didn't want the window to be too strong, because there would be many other pieces of art in the room. As it worked out, the window is still a strong focus.

In this window the linear background is disrupted by other shapes: portions of several concentric circles in the center, torn-looking shapes, twisted ribbon shapes. The window is almost divided into vertical thirds by two upright white lines. Although there is a concentration of activity in the window's center, the red line migrating from the linear background to the irregular foreground allows the eye to move easily from top to bottom (or vice versa). Jekyll chose red because it was Mrs. Wigle's favorite color. He used a lot of clear glass in this window in order to incorporate a view of the yard outside into the over-all effect.

Complex geometry figures more strongly in Robert Jekyll's work than in the work of many contemporary stained-glass artists. To rely on geometry might sound like a riskless approach to design, but Jekyll's use of it is never predictable or safe. In much of Jekyll's work, lines are pulled out of sync, elements are interjected, shapes are intriguingly shifted out of phase. These design procedures relate to a prime esthetic interest of the artist. "If I had to put my present interest down in one word, it would be *contrast*," Jekyll remarks. "I like to see straight lines or geometric lines interspersed and broken up with organic shapes. I like to see transparency contrasted with opacity. I like to see color juxtaposed with no-color. If you're intensifying anything in the human experience, it's through contrast."

In the independent panel *Aveugle Venitien* (See Plate 8), we see a somewhat more restrained contrast of line. Jekyll describes the piece as "a solitary event," in that, unlike many of his works, it is not part of a series. With a strong over-all verticality, the piece explores a shifting contrast of tone and texture. To achieve this, Jekyll used many different types of glass in the panel. It is a "a window of a window," as he puts it, because the idea for it came from a photograph Jekyll had taken in France, a photo of a house window that oddly had both curtains and venetian blinds. The window was broken, and a portion of a curtain was blowing out through a place where part of a pane was missing. The form of this photographed window offered a point of departure for the design of this panel, whose title translates as "Venetian Blindman."

Jekyll actually doesn't make many independent pieces. He expresses mixed feelings — and some definite reservations — about creating such "exhibition panels," as he likes to refer

PLATE 8: *Aveugle Venitien*, 1978.
35 × 41 in. (88.9 × 104.1 cm)
Collection of David Wilde.

to them. He feels that the independent panel, as an art form, might actually be dying a slow death because it's not being curated or collected on any significant scale. "I've sold some exhibition panels in the most surprising situations. It's arguable that a different type of market has to be created or stimulated for independent panels. But nobody has yet, to my knowledge, figured out how that market works." It may, he says, be inappropriate and impractical for stained-glass artists to, in effect, covet the painting's niche in the art marketplace. At root, it seems, Jekyll feels that stained glass is properly an architectural art form. "Architectural art is art that's complicated from the standpoint of displaying in galleries. But I question whether the independent panel, as an art form of its own, works. Is it sculpture, a painting, or *what* is it? It's a hybrid at best."

Nevertheless, he does feel that there is a legitimate function for such panels. "I think there's a role for the independent panel as an experimental field for artists to work out their ideas."

The Farrell residence (*See* Plate 9) contains another example of Jekyll's decided preference: work designed for a specific setting and function. The client's house was renovated, and what used to be the living room became the new kitchen. Jekyll was commissioned to design a window for the room. "The clients wanted something that would give them a degree of privacy without blocking their vision entirely. Beyond that, they were happy to let me do what I wanted. I bore in mind that the kitchen was painted predominantly gray. Also, I wanted the window to look good from the outside, so I picked up some of the architectural features of the building. The idea of the lenses set into the square, acid-etched areas came from some features of the pediment at the front of the house."

This three-part window epitomizes much of Robert Jekyll's work, as we've seen it, through the mid-1980s. With its density of composition combined with its mixed shapes and intersecting textural fields, it is reminiscent of Synthetic Cubist painting and collage. It has a joyous superabundance: multiple, jostling worlds, all eager to come forth at once. Perhaps what keeps this particular piece from being simply too much is the agreeable balance of cool and warm hues.

How does Jekyll know when one of his windows "works"? An answer to this question is always difficult to articulate, but Jekyll's is one of the best we've heard: "It's an over-all gut feeling as to whether your intentions have been met. Does it manipulate the light the way you wanted it to? Does it complement the interior the way you wanted it to? A piece may fail on some scores and exceed your expectations on others — which may have an effect on subsequent work, of course."

Obviously, many things, especially an artist's recent experimental work, contribute to the direction of new work. Long-standing influences, as well, are often significant. Besides Patrick Reyntiens, Jekyll cities as influences on his early work the painterly windows of John Piper, the colorful work of the British Romantic School, and the work of some of the contemporary German masters — particularly Wilhelm Buschulte — that he has studied *in situ*. However, Jekyll has long since enfolded these influences within himself and followed his own path. These days, he says, the germ of an idea can come from any number of sources. "Sometimes it can be an exhibition. I remember going to an exhibition some years ago of the Norwegian painter Edvard Munch's work. I went back to the show about three times. Every so often you see an exhibition and you can't wait to get back to the studio to start working. It sets off all kinds of ferment. Or you'll have some kind of visual experience — seeing a building or a movie — that makes you want to get your sketchbook out."

With respect to the process of developing the working designs from which he has fabricated his windows, Jekyll has used a couple of approaches. Some of his earlier work started off as watercolor sketches. He describes watercolor as a very fast, flexible approach that allows the artist to be exploratory — with the capability of producing ten or fifteen quick, tentative sketches in an hour. More recently, however, he has begun his designs with line — that is, by drawing — with only "subliminal" notions of color. He finds that this approach allows him to resolve decisively a problem more quickly. Often, line, especially straight line, is of fundamental importance to Jekyll's designs. "My work is architectural," he comments, "and in architecture you're dealing with linear situations; so, to me, somewhere there's got to be a linear reference." After he establishes the lines of a design, he often makes photocopies of his sketch and then experiments with color on a number of these copies. Some designs evolve from an initial casual doodle, while some are more deliberate in origin, requiring considerable research to provide the appropriate conceptual background or to spark visual ideas.

Keeping one's art alive is always a challenge. Jekyll manages to stay in touch with other glass artists in Europe as well as elsewhere in North America. He believes that isolation leads to indifferent art, and this is one of the reasons he has believed so strongly in the value of Artists in Stained Glass and other, similar organizations. He feels that workshops led by artists from outside Canada promote the sense of an international stained-glass community, as well as filling their more obvious function of providing learning environments for their participants. He has made it a point to study, from time to time, in Europe or in Canada with some master of stained glass whose work interests him.

Jekyll himself is familiar with the role of teacher. Between 1975 and 1982 he taught stained-glass courses, through Sheridan College's School of Crafts and Design and other venues. A number of the artists represented in this book were students of his at one time. The benefit of this teaching experience has been mutual, according to Jekyll. "I found that teaching tends to force you out of being stuck in one particular technique. Just to give the students an opportunity to know what they can do in different techniques, you tend to get involved with them yourself. In teaching your students, you teach yourself."

Where does Jekyll feel his work might be going from here?

"I'm concerned with the qualities of glass as they relate to light — in terms of reflection and refraction, various types of opacities, and so on," he says. "I'll continue to explore my time-honored preoccupation with different types of glass that are not traditionally associated with stained glass. And for a long time I've been thinking of working with glass block in creations, always trying to anticipate possible architectural applications. I've envisaged an installation in a gallery using glass block, and a stained-glass design would be integral with it. I'm also interested in taking old pressed pieces of glass and working them into a contemporary design."

Robert Jekyll's work is nothing if it is not a strong, distinctive, adventurous statement in glass. He has left his mark on the history of Canadian stained glass — first as an artist, and secondly as an organizer and teacher.

The work makes the artist. It is the evidence of his compelling urge to create.

PLATE 9: Farrell residence, 1982. 50 × 84 in. (127.0 × 213.4 cm) Toronto, Ontario. R.J.

Michael Anstead

In the past, Michael Anstead has been a computer operator, a concrete inspector, an architectural draftsman, a world traveler, and a tour guide in Africa. As a stained-glass artist of seven years' standing, Anstead says that he has sometimes felt as though life had reserved him, ultimately, for a stained-glass career. Interviewing him in Montreal, where he lives, we realized that he was utterly devoted to his artwork.

Anstead's initial interest in stained glass was sparked in 1977 by a friend who dabbled in the medium. Initially Anstead, too, was interested in stained glass only as a pastime. But he came to the medium with an inquisitive and self-reliant nature. Before long his involvement with stained glass had engendered a passionate enthusiasm for art in general. Anstead embarked on a wide-ranging study of historical and technical information pertaining to stained glass, both through library research and travel. He took a summer course with Robert Jekyll at Sheridan College's School of Crafts and Design and studied drawing for a time with Lise-Hélène Larine. Anstead's appetite for books on design and color became voracious, and he began to spend a lot of time in museums. In short, he undertook the art education he would need to pursue stained glass seriously. "It was necessary for me to become aware of what I like in art, so that I could then do my own things, from the heart."

Anstead bypassed the fascination with Art Nouveau styles common to novices in stained glass; such work involved the cutting of more pieces than he cared, or saw any reason, to do. He liked the grace of Victorian glass, however. Anstead had a lot of opportunity to study Victorian windows closely because he would take them on as repair jobs. "The first windows of my developing style were sort of 'asymmetrical Victorian'—things a little unexpected in something that would ordinarily be symmetrical." Within a fairly short time of his

MICHAEL ANSTEAD 49

introduction to stained glass, he was producing a lot of windows and independent panels.

With time, Anstead's work has become less purely decorative. The things he does have become personal visual statements in the form of architectural glass or independent panels. His views on autonomous stained-glass panels are interesting: "Certainly independent panels are valid from the artist's point of view, because they're probably the most challenging, the most up-front and interesting thing to do. But in terms of 'the world out there,' they are sort of orphans looking for homes."

Historical Romance (*See* Plate 10) is a good example of Anstead's independent panels. It has an over-all upbeat feeling, a luminous verve — as though the calligraphic gesture in the center were made of neon tubing. The panel "works" by virtue of its elegant simplicity. The rectangular leadline grid pattern in the background has yellow glass circles at all but one of the nodes of intersection; a single red circle at bottom center serves to balance the calligraphy that sits slightly above the panel's median line. The neon effect was brought about by the artist's having sandblasted the blue glass areas immediately surrounding the curving lead configuration.

Though some viewers have felt there is an unmistakable Japanese influence in his work, Anstead maintains that if he and the Japanese have arrived at similar esthetic destinations, it is sheerly coincidental. In any case, the calligraphic elements in some of his panels are strictly visual elements, having no intended or known meaning in any language; it's purely a matter of design. "I've often done things in my work and only afterwards tried to figure out why I did them and what I liked about them," Anstead explains. Like many artists, he

PLATE 10: *Historical Romance,* 1980. 12 × 24 in. (30.5 × 61 cm) Collection of artist.

J.R.

is basically intuitive in his approach to his work.

Anstead's ideas have often developed from offhanded doodles he has made. Another contributing source of ideas has been a process of esthetic exploration through photography. This process has involved his analyzing why he chose to take certain photos, in an attempt to sharpen his eye and to discover esthetic principles that he can use in his glass design. He also keeps notebooks of design ideas and saves sketches to refer to and learn from in the future.

"Some lines I've used in windows have come out of life drawing, and they're kind of secret because they're not used representationally. Only *I* know where they've come from." Often he juxtaposes this kind of organic line against a simple geometry or pattern of straight lines. The contrast between rational order and the organic order of the natural world fascinates Anstead. He sees a harmony between the apparent order and disorder, a harmony that has both tension and power in it.

Anstead tends to think first in terms of line, and to add color later. As a rule his designs are non-figurative. "Nonrepresentational work is very appealing to me; it's what I like to do. I set out to get a certain feeling in visual terms. A few years ago I wanted to do something distinctly musical, but I didn't want to include musical symbols. It turned out quite abstract, yet the first people who saw it said, 'Gee, this looks like music.' Usually I'm trying to evoke a specific mood."

Anstead must invest himself deeply in the basic idea of a piece before he can begin to work with it graphically. Once the idea really jells, he proceeds to a series of rudimentary sketches, which may in turn modify the initial concept. From this process a final design emerges. With autonomous panels, he relishes the freedom to change the design further as he proceeds with the construction stage. With commissioned architectural work, of course, the situation is quite a bit different. "After approval of a design by a client, I like to have ten percent room for change. Then I enjoy the construction process more, because I don't feel locked in; I feel like I'm still creating the window."

To date, Anstead's architectural work has been almost entirely residential. He's done much of this work in cooperation with interior designers. "I always say it's amazing what you can do with $40,000 and good taste," he quips with characteristic wry humor.

The foyer window that Anstead made for the Zunenshine residence (*See* Plate 11) was commissioned as part of a coordinated interior-design effort carried out by Mario Vissa of Montreal. Anstead got the idea for a sea-wave motif by considering the requirement of carrying the color of the turquoise carpet into the window. The free and natural form of the wave introduces a pleasantly exciting contrast to the rectangular forms of the living room, as well as to the outside and inside foyer windows and the door frame against which the wave "breaks." Anstead exercised an admirable restraint in this window, for the Zunenshine living room contains many art objects, and an over-elaborate design could easily have conflicted with these. The wave form is set against a simple background of horizontal bands of turquoise and white glass below and lots of clear "antique" glass above.

Anstead cut the streaky white glass so that its visual grain conforms to, and emphasizes, the surge of the wave. The clear glass allows a substantial amount of untinted natural light to enter the living room along with the turquoise light. Anstead used glass jewels and thinly sliced pieces of agate to simulate bubbles of splashing water. "The agates give the window a

PLATE 11: Interior entranceway, Zunenshine residence, 1983.
7 × 9 ft. (2.13 × 2.74 m)
Montreal, Quebec.

J.R.

nice organic feel. And I do like to have little points of interest at eye level in windows. If you're going through the door, you can enjoy the agates up close," the artist says. All the straight lines in the window are strong, rigid, zinc cames, while the curved lines were done using lead cames. Anstead designed the window to "read" nicely in the evening, when it would reflect light from the house's interior light sources, rather than be illuminated by light from outside.

Anstead's studies in stained glass, and art generally, continue. He participated in the workshop German glass-designer Jochem Poensgen led in Toronto in 1983, and in the one led by Johannes Schreiter in 1984. And he keeps abreast of developments in the stained-glass field through journals, books, slide shows, and exhibitions. However, he doesn't mention any well-known stained-glass artists as being of special importance in the evolution of his art. "Most of my favorite artists are personal friends," he says. "I know what they have struggled through."

Anstead expresses an uncommonly tolerant, even positive view of stained glass's popularity with hobbyists. "It's an interesting hobby for people. The more people there are who are aware of the processes and can do them, the more people there will be who can appreciate good work. I think there will be more and more people to support exhibitions."

While he is deeply devoted to stained glass and is consistently involved with it at one level of intensity or another, the degree of his diligence varies from week to week. But, he points out, the process of observation and learning is ceaseless. "It's all one," he declares. "One's life and one's artwork are the same. In a sense, I'm never working; and, in a sense, I'm always working."

Ernestine Tahedl

JOEL RUSS

Ernestine Tahedl grew up "next to the glass box." She was born in Austria during World War II, and was an only child. Her father was architectural-glass designer Heinrich Tahedl, and her mother was born to a family of stained-glass artisans. It is natural, then, that her earliest memories are as much of stained glass as they are of the Austrian countryside in which the family resided. When she was seven the family moved to Vienna. Ernestine remembers that, as she got older, her father gradually drew her, little by little, into his glass-design work.

"At first it was just little errands around the studio. Then slowly he got me more interested in designing, as well. Just before I left for Canada we were more or less equal partners in designing. My father left about eighty percent of the choosing of the glass to me, even if it was his design." There was never any question in the Tahedl family that Ernestine would also be an artist.

Tahedl's education was unusual. After her father showed a folio of his daughter's drawings to some members of the faculty of the Academy of Fine Arts in Vienna, she was immediately accepted as a student, though she was only fourteen years old at the time. Because the other students at the academy were of the usual post-secondary, art-school age, she became something of a loner. After six years of study at the academy, she graduated from its Master Class in Graphic Arts.

Though Tahedl's studies at the academy centered on print-making, she has always been an all-round artist. After graduation, while still living in Austria, she collaborated with her father on stained-glass windows for seven churches and two bank buildings. In 1963, the same year she left for Canada, Tahedl won a bronze medal at the Vienna International Exhibition of Paintings.

PLATE 12: (Overleaf) Sisters of the Holy Cross Chapel, 1964. 14 windows, each approx. 5 ft. (1.52 m) per side. Edmonton, Alberta. *Photograph by Joel Russ.*

What made her decide to emigrate to Canada? "Adventure!" she says, with a characteristic burst of merriment. While she was still in the academy, the artist Ernest Lindner, a visiting adult student from Canada, was a member of her printmaking class. "The instructor told him that if he wanted to know something, he should 'ask that girl over there, she usually knows the techniques,' " Tahedl recalls. "We struck up a friendship. He suggested that they could use someone like me in Canada. I just laughed it off and forgot about it until two years later, when I realized that becoming 'somebody' in the Austrian art scene would take a very long time."

Tahedl's father had a friend in Edmonton whose wife needed some help on a mural commission. So Ernestine left Austria with one trunk and no English. She was not intending to stay in Canada, but simply wanted to see what was here. "That was how I came to Canada. It worked out with the family, but the mural commission fell through. I had no money to go back to Austria." But after a short while, she had an exhibition of paintings in Edmonton, which is said to be the first exhibition of abstract work in that city. Soon, as well, she began to get commissions for stained-glass work.

In 1964 Tahedl was commissioned to design and make fourteen triangular windows for the chapel in the Sisters of the Holy Cross convent in Edmonton (*See* Plate 12). The design of the room was quite modern and spare, and the window openings were placed high in the exterior walls of the chapel. Tahedl handled this early commission quite nicely, using the traditional leaded technique.

In the daytime the windows are a lilting play of luminous shape and color that give the chapel a jubilant atmosphere. In these windows we see the varied palette that characterizes Tahedl's early work. The shapes of the leaded designs are formed by intersecting patterns of straight lines and arcs, with heavy dark lines around some shapes providing a feeling of depth.

Tahedl has always loved the intrinsic qualities of glass, and although she has tended in her later work to use fewer colors in a given piece than she did at Holy Cross, she has no qualms about strong hue. Her work has always tended toward a certain lyricism of form, and this particular esthetic inclination showed up rather early in her artistic development, before she left Austria.

Tahedl had, of course, seen the stained glass of various styles and eras in the churches of Austria. Her father introduced her to work of all kinds that he liked, not only stained glass but the work of modern painters and old European masters, as well. Teachers at the academy introduced her to Bauhaus ideas, and to Kandinsky. But Tahedl's personal esthetic leanings were toward the quiet, strong work of post-war abstract painters Alfred Manessier and Pierre Soulages.

Tahedl and her father were aware of the developments in post-war German stained glass but were never very influenced by them. Moreover, Austria — a smaller country — did not nurture anything like the stained-glass renaissance that took place in Germany. What happened in Austrian stained glass was minor compared to what happened after the war in German glass. "There was not that much philosophy around," Tahedl says of the post-war period. "People just tried to recuperate from the war; the artistic schools and philosophies came later." Perhaps this, as much as anything, is the reason that Tahedl's work evolved devoid of any influence from the streams of post-war glass design that are well known in North America. Accustomed to being a loner, when she left Austria at the age of twenty-three, Tahedl had already developed the strong artistic direction that is evidenced in the Sisters of the Holy Cross windows. She has followed her own path ever since.

Tahedl has always worked non-representationally in glass. "The thematic aspect of stained glass is really secondary. It's more a matter of a statement in colors," Tahedl says. "The figurative aspect of Chartres is nonexistent if you just step back a few meters — whereas later on, when you get into the Renaissance, it gets very figurative. Personally, I feel that with the Renaissance stained glass was in decline for many centu-

E.T.

ries." Tahedl was referring to the often-cited problem of integrating pictorial realism in glass into architectural structures.

Although she is extremely adept in both stained glass and painting, Tahedl is reluctant to compare the two art forms. She thinks of stained glass *per se* (as opposed to sculpture using glass, which she has also done) as an environmental art form that requires an artist to learn some very different lessons from those the painter must learn. She holds, for example, that a glass artist who knows his or her business can design a window that, when installed, will change the apparent proportions of a room to a considerable extent.

When doing architectural work, Tahedl takes stock of the givens involved in the building; and she actually relishes the challenge these constraints offer. Color and form are involved in her design process from the start, just as they are when she paints. "When designing stained glass, I start out with colored transparent cellophane, and I just play around with it until I get some shapes and forms that satisfy me. I have never really analyzed what I am doing in my artwork—not in painting, not in printmaking, and not in stained glass." Still, she feels that an interesting design always has a certain visual tension. To say that she is not analytical in her approach to design is certainly not to say that she isn't aware of her esthetic goals.

Over the years, Tahedl's stained glass has shown a movement toward simplification of composition and color range, a tendency foreshadowed in her *dalle de verre* (slab glass and concrete) work from the mid-sixties on. In painting, she starts out extremely bright, then tones the canvas down with glazes until she is satisfied that she has controlled the effect properly. She feels a degree of restraint is likewise called for in

PLATE 13: Mendel Art Gallery, 1970. 3 panels, each 4 × 10 ft. (1.22 × 3.05 m) Saskatoon, Saskatchewan.

stained glass. "I like to have the element of control in my designs," she says. "I've always been drawn to bring a certain serenity to any building. Less is more in a design, sometimes. Anybody can use a bit of serenity and quietness."

In her understanding of architectural-glass techniques, Tahedl probably has one of the most well-rounded backgrounds in contemporary Canadian stained glass. She has, of course, used the traditional leaded construction approach. She has also repeatedly used the *dalle de verre* technique in sizable architectural installations in buildings constructed of concrete. A technique she has worked with frequently, for both architectural work and free-standing sculpture, is lamination (or "cold-bonding") of antique glass to a plate-glass base, using epoxy resin. In Austria — in keeping with long-standing European practice — Tahedl and her father sent their window designs and selected glass to a glass craftsman for fabrication of the actual window, and she hasn't acquired much of a taste for leading since she came to Canada. The laminating approach has allowed her a quicker method of construction, as well as somewhat greater flexibility in terms of visual effect.

At the Mendel Art Gallery in Saskatoon (*See* Plate 13), Tahedl used the cold-bonding glass-appliqué technique in making some very interesting three-dimensional windows. The givens in the situation were, simply, the lengthy expanse of plate glass against which Tahedl's pieces would be situated, and the curtains. In each piece, colored antique glass has been applied to a four-by-ten-foot (1.2 m × 3 m) structure, made from manufactured glass U-channels, that acts as a strong three-dimensional armature. The three glass-channel structures are affixed to floor and ceiling.

Each of the three windows is unique, though all are made with the same assortment of antique glass. Each is a complex variation on the same theme, combining arc shapes with ribbon-like bands that appear to interweave. There is an interesting handling of negative and positive space in the composition of these windows, an imaginative use of the contrast between the antique glass and the transparent structural glass that supports it. The various red and orange hues impart an interesting depth to the design. In each window the constituent shapes of the design are basically geometric and simple, but the total effect has a dynamic quality that is partly due to the three-dimensional nature of the object. These windows were the point of departure for Tahedl's exploration of actual, free-standing glass sculpture.

The Bibliothèque Municipale de Varennes, in Varennes, Quebec (*See* Plate 14), contains another — and quite powerful — example of Tahedl's use of the appliqué technique. By the repetition of arc shapes in a variety of relationships to one another, the window's design plays on the shape of the semi-circular entranceway ceiling that the window sits below. Here the spaces between the pieces of antique glass lend the purfled effect that the leadlines do in traditional stained glass — but in reverse: instead of blocking the sunlight, they allow it through unfiltered. These cutlines within and between arc shapes give the design a subtle dimension of complexity it would not have if the colored arcs were unsegmented.

There is no rusticity, no lack of sophistication in Tahedl's work. Yet, although the artist spent quite a number of years living in Vienna, Edmonton, and Montreal, she is most at home in the country. It is the environment in which she spent her earliest years. Her present home, in rural King City, outside Toronto, undoubtedly has a definite influence on her current artwork. "I feel, even in an abstract design, that I still try to capture the serenity of the country," she confides. "It may seem far-fetched, but I would say my inspiration is

E.T.

PLATE 14: Bibliothèque Municipale de Varennes, 1982. 6 × 12 ft. (1.83 × 3.66 m) Varennes, Quebec.

nature. I've always been happiest in the country."

Tahedl works daily in her pleasant, well-outfitted studio. She has a specially designed sunlit glass easel on which she works out her designs. Starting work early in the day, she usually quits around 3 P.M., when the light begins to wane. Her partiality for natural lighting has meant that she has never been very happy with artificial backlighting for her stained glass. Fortunately, most of her work has been installed in situations that have allowed the natural backlighting of sunlight.

When working on an architectural commission, Tahedl usually spends time in her studio playing with four or five different initial design possibilities at once. Choosing the one that she feels is best, she presents it to the client. If the client doesn't care for it, she will start over again rather than go back to designs she has previously rejected. Each design effort thus receives her devoted attention.

Tahedl's artwork has received substantial acclaim over the years. Her paintings and prints have been shown and collected internationally, and she has enjoyed considerable success with the stained-glass work she has done here in Canada. Among the many honors and awards she has received have been a commission to design glass for the Sanctuary in the Canadian Pavilion at Expo 67, in Montreal, and her election to the Royal Canadian Academy of the Arts in 1977. Of course, as fulfilling as such accomplishments are, these are not where the chief enjoyment of working in art lies for her. "It's not the installation of the piece or the pats on the back that I enjoy, but that feeling of satisfaction of achieving harmony between a couple of tonalities, for example. It's just a moment, but it's a high you want to repeat. Stained-glass artists work darn hard, and it would be a shame if we missed those moments of pleasure."

Ken MacDonald

like what I like in any school of art. What I appreciate is the ability of an artist, who has sweated over his work, to make it appear very easy—the capricious result of a career of intense application.''

Ken MacDonald reveals himself with this statement. For while he favors a nonchalant, if energetic, feeling in his work, he has not shrunk from the years of personal application that for an artist are the substance of a good background. MacDonald pursued some of his learning formally; he attended university off and on from 1969 onward, studying English and French literature, art history, and the history of architecture, as well as taking studio art courses in drawing and sculpture. But he has taken some lengthy breaks from formal education to pursue other types of life experience, as well. When we interviewed him, he was completing work toward a degree in fine arts.

MacDonald describes himself as a basically restless person who had trouble focusing on any one thing until he discovered stained glass. While a university student in Victoria, B.C., in 1969, he became interested in the medium. His mother had pursued painting as an avocation while he was growing up, but he himself did not enter university with any particular interests in art. Initially what he saw in stained glass was much less a medium for self-expression than a craft he might practice in order to take control of his economic circumstances. He set up a studio with two friends, and the three of them went into production doing Tiffany-style lamps and other readily salable items. After a few years, MacDonald left the partnership to continue working on his own.

In 1974, looking back to time he had spent in Paris in 1967, he decided that he would like to live in France for an extended period. In part, MacDonald was attracted by the French people

PETER DUTHIE

and culture; in part, he wished to pursue the interest in Gothic architecture that he had developed while a student. He also felt that a change of scene — an adventure — would be stimulating for him personally and artistically. He decided that this move might be more feasible if he were to develop sufficient expertise in stained glass to take with him a truly viable trade. It was a couple of years before he felt prepared, and, during this period, he took a number of university-level art courses.

In 1976 MacDonald moved to the south of France, settling in Beausoleil, near Nice. Here he established a stained-glass studio where he worked until his return to Canada in 1982. When MacDonald moved to France, he was competent at stained-glass construction but, in his own estimation, not yet artistically original or inspired. Working on commercial commissions, he was able to finance a lifestyle that involved study, travel, leisure, and getting to know some artists who were doing interesting things. He worked a great deal through interior-design firms, who contracted him to do work for various sorts of buildings, including restaurants, nightclubs, and piano bars. Mostly the work was made to order. Only occasionally did MacDonald have a client who let him exercise his imagination. As he became better established, he began to get commissions in other countries, shipping glass work to places such as Brazil, Switzerland, and Spain. Yet the opportunity to do large-scale, original work — to really stretch himself artistically — eluded him virtually all the while he lived in France.

The first chance MacDonald had to do something really original came in 1980 through the artist's older brother, an architect. The owner of Notre Dame Place, an office building in Calgary, wanted to put some artwork in the

building's lobby. MacDonald flew back to Canada to pursue the opportunity. He learned that the client simply wanted something "different and impressive." Returning to France, MacDonald came up with a design, which he submitted. The design was accepted.

Illumined from behind with artificial light, the Notre Dame Place panel (*See* Plate 15) certainly adds something pleasant to what would otherwise be a rather plain lobby. To us, its forms suggest a tropical environment, perhaps something like the plant life on a swamp's edge. "The shapes are familiar, even though you can't identify them. They're organic," MacDonald comments. "I used muted colors. The background color is sky blue. The elements are mostly a mixture of grays and green-grays. There's movement and balance, but there's tension, because it's all just a *little* out of balance."

There is something quite characteristic of MacDonald's current work in the carefree composition of this panel. While living on the south coast of France, MacDonald became fascinated with Mediterranean art. This interest actually became a passion, and MacDonald feels that he absorbed a good deal of the Mediterranean sensibility from the place, its people, and its art. Today MacDonald sees artists like Joan Miro and Jean Dubuffet, with their playful approaches, as his major influences. Wassily Kandinsky, the most celebrated of the founders of abstract painting, has been another important influence on MacDonald. While Kandinsky lived most of his life in his native Russia and in Germany, as a child he traveled in Italy with his parents, and while a young man he was exposed to the whimsical, often garishly colored folk art of

PLATE 15: Notre Dame Place, 1981. 8 × 12 ft. (2.44 × 3.66 m) Calgary, Alberta.

J.R.

the Vologda region. Perhaps such influences, along with Kandinsky's commitment to an extreme subjectivity, account for a sensibility that MacDonald views as compatible with the Mediterranean.

Sometimes these influences on MacDonald's design work are readily apparent. In 1982 the artist was commissioned to design a large, built-in panel for the inner lobby of the Emerson Centre in Calgary (*See* Plate 16). "This is the piece I've had the most freedom with," MacDonald says. "It was commissioned without a design first being accepted, which put a tremendous responsibility on me. I worked harder on this than on any other design." In this delicately orchestrated visual tumult, we see something of the playful randomness of Miro's composition combined with something of the energy and abstraction of Kandinsky's.

"The colors are distinct, yet they harmonize," MacDonald points out. "The background is white, which makes all the colors stand out. It's lyrical, musical. It expresses me and my six years of living on the Mediterranean, and it relates to nothing else in the lobby. Luckily there *is* nothing else in the lobby, so it doesn't have to." This time, as well, the panel is artificially lit. It is made from semi-opaque glass backed with diffusion material, both serving to even out the illumination.

MacDonald remarks that he enjoys the ambiguity of the forms in this panel, the fact that the viewer may immediately and unconsciously project interpretations on them — in other words, "identify" them. He likes, in fact, to work with forms that are at the most distant point they can be from anything objective without losing a hint of the familiar.

With the arrival of the Emerson Centre commission, Mac-Donald moved back to Canada, setting up business in Victoria, B.C. His recent work is the curious product of an artist who is preoccupied with self-expression yet is drawn to the challenge of architectural work. "In architectural stained glass, you have to consider everything around you. But I've been lucky in a couple of commissions where I've had nothing but a blank wall in a boxlike space to deal with. So within those pieces I expressed myself," he says. "If an architectural situation allows me to be lyrical and capricious, then I will. But if the situation has some rather definite personalities involved — clients with definite tastes — then I hunker down and express myself through those personalities."

MacDonald's predilection is to approach stained-glass design almost as a painter approaches his canvas, and though the outcome of the process appears casual, he in fact labors intensely over his designs. "When I do a design, it has to work whether it's right side up, upside down, or sideways," he reveals. "Balance comes through tension," he continues. "I would rather slightly irritate someone visually than massage them."

To keep "in shape" for designing, MacDonald says, "I draw and sketch a lot. If on the surface it doesn't seem to influence my work, under the surface it must. I guess I work on *myself* that way. You can't find anything more worth drawing than the human form. And for a while I got into drawing abstractions of human and animal skulls. You wouldn't have known that these drawings were skulls, but the organic abstraction was intriguing."

Art is an adventure for MacDonald that presents to him a boundless horizon. "I'm happy in not being happy with what I've done. In art there's no retirement, no end in sight. I'll never accomplish 'it.' I can always improve. I haven't found myself checked in what I want to do in stained glass. The potential is limitless."

PLATE 16: (Overleaf) Emerson Centre, 1983. 23 × 11.5 ft. (7.01 × 3.51 m) Calgary, Alberta. *Photograph by Peter Duthie.*

Brian Hoyano

Glass is one of the main materials in cities. Because it is used *en masse*, as it is, we tune it out. Those anonymous towers. Glass is not itself characterless; it's what's been done with it. What I like about glass are things like its clarity, its translucence, the very pure, pristine surface sheen, and the hard geometry. I like to emphasize those qualities of glass, and at the same time maybe make it a bit more human, because it is so often a dehumanizing aspect of urbanity."

There is always a human element in Brian Hoyano's work, even when the design is a highly site-determined one. His windows and panels are precarious, inconstant, vulnerable — like people. Hoyano is incessantly taking esthetic risks, and the most intimate examples of his work are often fascinating because of a ticklishly poised quality this venturesomeness imparts to the designs. Indeed, the appeal of his windows and panels is often to be found in their gamely conjectural visual character.

The Hoyano signature is clear in the front-door window the artist made for the Sly residence in Vancouver (*See* Plate 17). The clients wanted a window that would be a faithful expression of the artist's spirit and also fulfill a couple of their own requirements. One stipulation was that the window both admit light and provide privacy. And because the house is located in a predominantly Chinese neighborhood, the clients wanted something with an Oriental flavor.

Hoyano constructed the window using the glass-appliqué technique. A background pattern was provided by sandblasting closely spaced horizontal bands on the clear foundation glass. Hoyano chose the fuchsia accent color, which he used very sparingly, because it approximates the exterior color of the house. The window's design has a whimsical, delicately balanced feeling to it. The composition is full of understated

tensions that animate it, yet there is a captivating fragility to the design.

This fragility has been a frequent ingredient in Hoyano's work. It would seem to relate closely to the theme of perishability that interests the artist. "I like the jagged line, the frenetic edge. When you're viewing antiquities, frequently they're not complete; although the original artist hadn't counted on that degradation occurring, it works — it offers a new entity that's interesting. I can be walking down the street and see a broken window, and not think too much about it. But in the course of my designing, that image may be recalled to me." Deterioration is the perennial concomitant of existence. What more apt medium than fragile glass could there be in which to explore such a profound theme?

Hoyano arrived at his present serious and philosophical involvement with glass work gradually. In 1979 he got his introduction to stained glass as a craft, and it was initially the colored shapes enclosed by the leadline that appealed to him. He took an introductory course in Vancouver and began to make boxes, lampshades, and so on. Realizing he was able to fashion such items more skillfully than many of those who were selling their wares at craft fairs, he decided he too might be able to make a living selling them. He quit his job and set up business. Before long he was making nonfunctional stained-glass panels, as well. As his experience grew, he raised the level of his goals, making serious efforts to improve his art. Soon he began to realize, to his dismay, that people in general did not make a distinction between good and bad art in stained glass, as they might in other media. He felt that this had an adverse effect on the general level of artistic quality in the medium as it was practiced in independent panels or residential work. With his own aims growing ever more earnest, he felt increasingly isolated from other people involved in stained glass. When he met Brian Baxter through the Vancouver-based Circle Craft Cooperative, he knew he had found a kindred spirit. "He gave me the encouragement to really be more critical about glass work, to compare it with other contemporary art forms," says Hoyano.

Some of Hoyano's early patrons required him to design work in Art Nouveau or Art Deco veins, although his personal interest did not rest for long with these period approaches to design and to the use of color. Hoyano sees such approaches in a historical perspective deriving from his general study of art history. He feels it is important to leave these dated approaches to the past, where they were appropriate, and he makes efforts to stay aware of contemporary trends in art. "Research is a large part of your creative task," he believes. "The artist who thinks he can create something just from inside himself is missing an important point. You're a

PLATE 17: Sly residence, 1983. 28 × 23 in. (71.1 × 58.4 cm) Vancouver, B.C.

J.R.

modern being. It's your complete environment that should influence how you express yourself."

According to Hoyano, the most glaring problem with the Art Nouveau look that so many people in North America associate with stained glass is that it is anachronistic; it is not compatible with modern urban architecture, and it doesn't express the contemporary cosmopolitan sensibility. With architectural glass, Hoyano is concerned that the design be appropriate to the architectural setting and to the needs of the people who use the building (often, in the case of his work, a residence). Of course, beyond this, he prefers situations that allow him to extend his esthetic explorations.

Hoyano's work in the entranceway of the Lotzker residence (*See* Plate 18) comprises an integrated set of windows framing the front door, with a single design running through all five panels. Here we see Hoyano's fascination with mutability and the ragged, "deteriorated" edge. The design's background is composed of wide sandblasted bands and a mixture of clear and colored glass in orderly, narrow bands that sometimes form squares by their intersection. This tidy background is rent by emerging patterns of various textures and colors.

While Hoyano's ongoing personal interest in the theme of mutability is apparent, the artist's design was meant to be a response to the personality of his client, whom he describes as "quite a happy person. The colors that I used are quite strong and tropical, in keeping with the personality of the person who commissioned the piece. Also," he continues, "I wanted to soften the background grid, and the way I did it was with the organic shapes and lines which twirl about each other and joyfully play in front of the grid." The end result of Hoyano's creative process here is very lively and pleasing.

In the windows and panels Hoyano refers to as his "erosion series," including the set in the Lotzker residence, one might infer the influence of the eminent post-war German glass designer, Johannes Schreiter, who pioneered the thematic exploration of disintegration in his own work. Indeed, although Hoyano has pursued his own meditations on this theme and made his own visual discoveries in relation to it, he counts Schreiter as an early influence on him. Other well-known contemporary glass artists whom Hoyano admires are Jochem Poensgen, another German, and Robert Kehlmann, an American. However, Hoyano is quick to point out that "the biggest mistake that glass artists make is to look to glass art for their inspiration. It's really quite stultifying."

Recently Hoyano's independent panels have taken a direction in which there are few precedents, and no famous practitioners. His panel *Trace 1* (*See* Plate 19) is a good example of this new work. The title derives from a series of works in which the artist has explored the idea of found traces of a wasted civilization—an industrial civilization much like our own, to judge by the materials the artist has used in the pieces. *Trace 1* was made from three large, roughly shaped pieces of wire-reinforced safety glass and many small bits of cut and broken clear glass cold-bonded to a piece of plate glass. The applied pieces have a suspended feeling, as though they still show evidence of some upheaval. The exceptional visual depth in the panel results from the fact that pieces of glass have been applied to both sides of the sandblasted foundation glass, and thus pieces on the opposite side from the viewer are seen somewhat indistinctly, almost in silhouette.

Hoyano's independent glass panels are moving into a radically non-traditional vein, both technically and, to an even greater extent, esthetically. Many of his current pieces involve no color at all, but instead use glass of varying degrees of translucence. The cold-bonding method allows him to laminate layers of glass and to retain the raw edge of roughly cut or broken glass. "The leadline has come to bother me more and more," he admits. "I still like the way it can look, but it means I have to completely enclose a shape, and I can do without that. I like the soft light of sandblasted glass, and a sharp edge of glass against this soft light."

A natural question with work of this nature is, Is it stained

glass?—and that's difficult to answer. In these pieces Hoyano employs many of the techniques—appliqué and sandblasting, for example—used in more recognizable, if non-traditional, forms of contemporary stained glass. The panels are translucent, and although the pieces have surface relief, they are not sculptural; the emphasis remains on the modulation of light, rather than on the manipulation of mass. Perhaps work such as this will one day be given its own category among *objets d'art*—receive its own label. But in the work of Brian Hoyano, it is clear that the pieces in question have gradually evolved from the most conventional forms of stained glass. That such work is being created at the periphery of stained glass's compass is an indication of just how vital the medium currently is.

PLATE 18: (Left) Lotzker residence, 1981. Total area approx. 27 sq. ft. (2.51 sq. m) Vancouver, B.C.

PLATE 19: (Below) *Trace 1*, 1983. 43 × 27 in. (109.2 × 68.6 cm) Collection of artist.

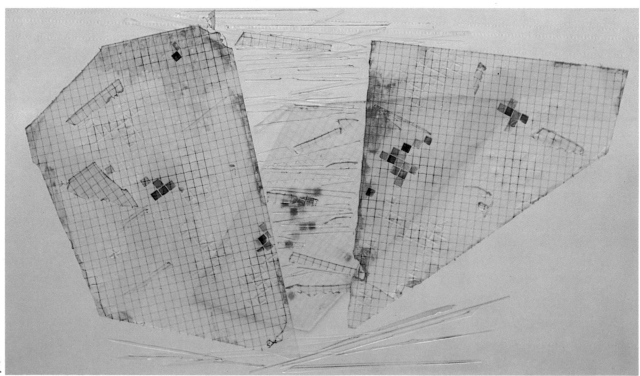

Lutz Haufschild

While he was a student at Hanover's Advanced Institute of Art and Technology, Lutz Haufschild discovered his aptitude for work of a monumental scale. "Most students could work well in small scale, but not in large scale. But with me it was just the opposite." The work Haufschild has done in western Canada constitutes some of the largest-scale architectural stained glass executed in North America to date. It is work that has evoked international acclaim in recent years.

When Lutz Haufschild arrived in Vancouver in 1967, he couldn't speak English well enough to ask his way around the city. He was a talented young man, with a solid art education acquired in his native Germany; even so, he was obliged by his lack of connections and reputation to eke out a living for a time as a house painter. By 1969, however, Haufschild was beginning to design significant public sculptural works in western Canada.

Haufschild was born and raised in Hanover. Until he was about twenty, he had not decided what direction his life would take. After high school he had wanted to study architecture. But in Germany an architecture student had first to study engineering, and Haufschild did not have an engineer's frame of mind. Just to see what would happen, he began studies at Hanover's Advanced Institute of Art and Technology.

Now, though he is critical of it in some respects, he counts his three-and-a-half-year course of study at the institute as one of the two most important factors in his accomplishments as an artist. "At that school you could have learned, for example, any painting style ever done anywhere in the world, with any kind of material. But some of the profs we had were very strict and narrow, and there was no room with them for your own interpretations: 'Do it this way, or don't do it at all.' Some of them were very dry and businesslike."

In terms of scope and esthetic philosophy, the institute was a spiritual successor to the Bauhaus. Among the techniques that Haufschild studied there were those of easel and fresco painting, of mosaic work, of sculptural and relief work, and of stained-glass work in the colorful French tradition. He feels that what he was taught very well was art history, a subject he especially enjoyed because he found quite intriguing the impact of factors like climate, technical developments, and politics on how people live and express themselves.

"At the Advanced Institute we were also encouraged to travel, to actually see the things we were taught about," Haufschild recalls. "During my years as a student I traveled to France and met Marc Chagall, while he was working on the Jerusalem windows, and I also met Le Corbusier. This was when I realized it was important to always seek out the best and talk to them."

Indeed, Haufschild identifies travel as the other great shaping influence in his life, something that has continued to be a source of education for him. Just after his graduation from the institute, he decided to leave northern Germany, whose winters he could no longer bear. He had considered moving to the south of the country but decided that, as the south was so different from the north, he might just as well go to another continent and have a real adventure. An old friend of his father had settled in Canada, so it was here he headed. After an ocean cruise to Halifax, he ultimately arrived in Vancouver, which was to become his home base.

By the time he left art school, Haufschild had acquired a sense of personal direction. "I wanted to work with buildings, with the environment, with works which were related to places, which would be meaningful to people, and which

PLATE 20: (Overleaf) Westminster Abbey, 1981. 82 windows totalling nearly 7000 sq. ft. (650.3 sq. m) Mission, B.C. *Photograph by Joel Russ.*

many would use." But it took a little while for the requisite opportunities to make themselves available to him in his adopted home.

As a temporarily unemployed house painter, in 1969, Haufschild entered and won a national competition for a commission to do a sculptural installation in the West Coast Transmission Building in Vancouver. Though he did his first self-directed, professional stained-glass work the next year, for a Seattle church, he viewed this glass work as a mere diversion from his real vocation. Haufschild's artistic reputation as a gifted creator of public sculptural work was, after all, just budding.

"I had done stained-glass work as a student, but I didn't take it as serious art," he recalls. "The thing about glass that I liked was that it always came out looking better than you had planned. You almost couldn't fail — which is the problem I have with a lot of stained glass you see now: no matter how badly it is done, it still seems to come out all right."

Despite the modest success Haufschild had had, at this point, in creating sculpture for public places, he wondered why some public spaces he had seen were well used by people, while others, though comparably financed and seemingly well designed, were not well liked. In hopes of doing more extensive firsthand research on the topic, he applied for a Canada Council grant to finance a year's worth of world travel. Perhaps partly because renowned architect Arthur Erickson and Vancouver Art Gallery director Tony Emery vouched for his worth with letters of appraisal, he was awarded the grant. In any case, he traveled to more than twenty countries — including Japan, Indonesia, India, Iran, Greece, Spain, Holland, and Mexico — during 1973–74.

When asked what he feels is the common denominator of good public or architectural art, he muses for a moment, then says, "It's very hard to define what it is in words. But I would say it has something to do with clarity of conception, with cultural significance, and with the care and attention put into it."

After his return to Canada, Haufschild spent a few years living in Whistler, B.C., a ski resort area north of Vancouver. Here he built a house that an architect designed for him using ideas Haufschild had brought back from his year of travel. When his house was destroyed by a fire, he built again, this time drawing up his own plans. "In school I had done readings in architecture, but designing my own house and then building it helped me to understand the relationship between the scale at which you design and what the thing actually turns out to be." He also designed several houses for other people. In this way Haufschild undoubtedly gained a greater understanding of the needs and practical concerns of architects, as well as of the problems and necessities of scale.

Through most of the 1970s Haufschild's focused energies went into abstract sculpture. His real debut in the world of serious stained-glass work came in 1979, when he was commissioned to design a 380-foot-long stained-glass skylight for a shopping mall in Coquitlam, B.C. He looks back on this as the point when he began to understand the potential stained glass held as a large-scale medium.

The next year presented Haufschild with the kind of opportunity that stained-glass artists dream of. A Benedictine monastery near Mission, in British Columbia's lower mainland area, had begun the construction of a large church, intended primarily for the brethren's own celebration of the liturgy. Based on a *crux quadrata* floor plan, the building designed by architect Ashbjorn Gathe would be one of the largest cast-in-place concrete buildings in North America. Its accordion-folded walls would accommodate sixty-four lancet windows, each twenty-two feet high, and its domed roof would contain twelve windows covering a thousand square feet.

The church in progress was sited on a lovely hill crest within the monastery grounds, so that light, direct and indirect, would pour in from all directions. Because the material used in constructing the building was cast concrete, and because of the immense scale of the fenestration — the total window area was to be nearly seven thousand square feet — Haufschild chose to use the *dalle de verre* (slab glass and concrete) approach. The sixty-four window openings in the walls were identical in size and shape. To provide the desired visual variety, as well as to provide the structural framework needed to stabilize the windows, Haufschild designed a sturdy tracery, to be cast in concrete, for each window opening. The configurations were developed from ten distinct modular patterns, each incorporating right-angled elements, that could be used repeatedly throughout all the windows — without loss of visual variation — by simply rotating the patterns 90 degrees or 180 degrees. Within this framework Haufschild chose to use small pieces of glass — squares, triangles, and rectangles—because this would allow for a gradation of color in the windows. The repeated shapes in the tracery and in the glass, along with the over-all gradation-of-color scheme, would lend a unifying factor to the design as a whole. This was of special importance in a situation where, because of the accordion-like walls, from certain angles only every second window would be visible.

In situ, the collective effect of these spires of glass definitely transcends their individuality; indeed, the effect is a thoroughly environmental one from certain vantage points within the building. The sun's rays enter the interior of the church as a flood of felicitous and inspiring light. Each of the quadrants of the building accommodates windows with a particular range of hues having a symbolic elemental value: blue for "water," red/yellow for "fire" (*See* Plate 20), violet for "air," and a color variegation giving an over-all brown impression for "earth." The first three of these sets of windows are arranged with their deeper, darker hues toward the bottom, and their lighter, more ethereal ones toward the top — with an intermingling of the two in the windows' middle sections. Without question, the total effect of this expansive church interior, with its high-vaulted ceiling and its sublime fenestration, is an emotionally uplifting one.

With stained glass Haufschild was getting the opportunities to work on a large scale that his art education in Hanover had prepared him for. The abbey in Mission, B.C., helped to establish his reputation solidly. Another major opportunity to work with flat glass in an expansive architectural setting came in 1982, in the form of Edmonton's Scotia Place office building, designed by that city's James B. Wensley & Associates.

The firm's architects had made a provision for a huge glass panel to be installed, in an aluminum frame, between the bottom of the second floor and the top of the fourth. They intended the stained glass to solve a major architectural problem: from the building's atrium, the upper portions of some rather unattractive, older, adjacent buildings were clearly visi-

PLATE 21: Scotia Place, 1982. 32 sq. ft. (2.97 sq. m) Edmonton, Alberta.

LUTZ HAUFSCHILD 91

ble through the thirty-three-foot-square window opening that admitted sunlight to the interior. To complicate the situation, shadows cast by these nearby buildings played havoc with the light coming in through this opening. The fact that a structural framework had already been designed when the artist was called in only served to make the constraints more limiting. Working with scale models, Haufschild coped with the dictates of this potentially conspicuous grid framework by using a bold design approach. This would work out happily; the scale and rectangularity of the setting, and of the window itself, called for a robust treatment rather than conspicuous intricacy of detail. Haufschild met the requirement of blocking the view of the buildings outside by choosing to use opak (semi-opaque) glass, with a band of very saturated hues crossing the panel diagonally. Having settled on his design, he contracted Freemont Antique Glass Company, in Seattle, to make handblown, flashed glass to his specifications. This was then cut and leaded into component panels by craftsmen at Kitsilano Stained Glass, in Vancouver, working under the artist's supervision. The design of the entire window incorporates a subtle leadline reticulation within the pronounced over-all pattern, the artist's intention being to lend a human scale to the colossal panel.

This commission was a most challenging one, not the least because the abundance of plate glass in the building would, by itself, tend to give the interior a cold, adamantine feeling. Besides hiding what would have been a dreary view of the adjacent buildings, the panel (*See* Plate 21), with its yellow and deep-red hues, succeeds admirably in lending the space a warmer and more congenial feeling. Haufschild's use of the bias in the design lends a much-needed contrast to the horizontal and vertical lines of the atrium, yet this is still an essentially geometric compositional approach that allowed Haufschild to keep his panel appropriate to the rectilinear masses of the architecture. The choice of saturated glass works well to overcome the light-and-shadow problem; the panel remains interesting even when it is not fully illuminated by direct sunlight.

After seeing this and other works by Haufschild, it becomes apparent what a protean artist he is. He has no "style" as such; in other words, it would be very difficult to identify a work of his on the basis of having seen other works he has done. His stained-glass designs are completely site-specific, based on a comprehensive consideration of the function and essential features of the place. In this insistence he evinces his philosophical kinship with the esteemed German glass designer Jochem Poensgen, whom he has assisted in teaching at the Pilchuck School of Glass in Washington State, as well as in Toronto and Germany.

Yet even when an artist is faced with compelling architectural givens, modern art remains a quest. That he has taken a highly site-specific approach does not mean that Haufschild has not invested himself in his designs; on the contrary, there is always room for the artist's individuality to come into play in a situation in the form of a creative solution. Haufschild's is an approach to architectural-glass design that is constantly evolving. Haufschild cites the empowering result of his own study at Pilchuck, in 1981, with that master of contemporary stained glass, Johannes Schreiter. "What Schreiter said to me was, 'Anything goes. If you have an idea, find a way of doing it; don't let the material dictate.' This was completely the opposite of the Bauhaus attitude I was taught at the Advanced Institute, that the material determines how you work with it. I was shocked and liberated at the same time."

Haufschild has certainly put Schreiter's advice to good use. When we interviewed him, his most recent work seemed to us to be his most impressive and inventive stained-glass accomplishment to date. It is the result of a 1983 commission to design fenestration for the Ismaili Jamatkhana ("prayerhouse" or "mosque") in Burnaby, B.C. "The mosque is the most thorough work I've done," Haufschild says. "I put more energy, more research, and more of my collected experience into that than any other project."

Although architecture has been by far the most important expression of religion in Islamic art, the Ismaili sect has built few edifices. The Ismaili community has been very much interested in revitalizing Islamic architecture. It has encouraged the development of a new architecture that would synthesize the requisites of contemporary life with considerations of Islamic faith and principles. Architect Bruno Freschi splendidly adapted traditional architectural elements to a building that is both contemporary in style and appropriate to the cool-weather climate of B.C.'s lower mainland. It was Freschi's task to impart a symbolically important expansive feeling to the interior of this relatively small mosque (approximately eleven thousand square feet on the ground floor) and to engender the time-honored Islamic sense of visual delight through an imaginative yet orderly manipulation of space. The building's windows were envisaged as an integral part of achieving these goals.

Freschi originally conceived the main windows as three-dimensional, almost lantern-like. Haufschild suggested a reversal of the original inward-projecting configuration, so that, as seen from the interior, the perimeter portion of the windows would sit approximately flush with the center of the wall plane, while the window's center portion would recede, or "expand" outwardly.

Another—and perhaps more important—area of consideration with respect to the design of the glass was related to the building's primary purpose. As with Christian churches, a prime requirement with the mosque was to create an environment that would seem detached from the rush and petty concerns of the external world. To a degree, this desired separateness would be fostered automatically by any building enclosed so as to cope with the climate. But beyond this lay the central matter of creating an essentially traditional flavor of the sacred — one devoid of iconography, statuary, ritual objects, and pews. Freschi utilized the principles of symmetry and geometry that are fundamental to Islamic architecture in evolving the basic building design and decorative surface-treatment elements. In this commission, Haufschild felt it was important to develop a clearly non-Christian stained-glass vocabulary.

The building's main windows needed, then, to insure seclusion, maintain the environmental mood, and properly modulate the incoming light. Haufschild chose to use one-inch-thick cast glass in these windows for two reasons: first, cast glass held in a steel frame would not carry the Christian associations that leaded glass would; second, thick glass would offer security advantages, as vandalism was feared. Haufschild remembered some silver-stained architectural glass he had seen in Europe with which he had been very much impressed, and he decided he would use silver staining to transfer a pattern onto cast glass. When inquiries to North American firms seemed to indicate that the silver-staining process he had in

PLATE 22: Burnaby Jamatkhana, 1984. Portion of entranceway screen; total area approx. 1000 sq. ft. (92.9 sq. m) Burnaby, B.C.

mind could not be used with cast glass, he located a firm in West Germany — the Hein Derix Studios — that sent him samples to prove that it *could* be done.

Haufschild drew upon his study of the arabesque marble screens at Fatehpur Sikri in India and of the Alhambra in Spain as background in the painstaking process of evolving his graphic-pattern conception; his glass would have to transmit a light similar in effect to the precious, monochromatic light admitted to those great, classic mosques by their screens. More specifically, it was necessary to make graphic reference to the fundamental design elements — the square and the octagon — that Bruno Freschi had elaborated upon in his architectural scheme.

Haufschild finally decided to use, as a primary pattern, an intersection of discontinuous lines that, over-all, would give the impression of squares within squares. It was a pattern that, while essentially simple, would suggest complexity. The central, three-dimensional section of each window would be made up of multiple sixteen-inch-square panes bearing this subtle design and held in place by a specially designed steel framework. This central section would be surrounded by a slightly bolder border pattern that echoed the primary design. Haufschild had the panes specially cast in one-inch opalescent glass by Wiesenthalhütte in Schwäbisch Gmünd, West Germany. On these slabs his patterns were silver-stained on both sides of the glass, in a rust shade, by the Hein Derix Studios of Kavalaer. He decided to have the stained pattern applied to both sides of the cast glass because he felt this would make the pattern read well from the outside of the building as well as from the inside; and because the double pattern would simulate the vibrant halation effect of light passing through the marble or wood screens of traditional mosques.

For the screen panels surrounding the front entrance doors (28), Haufschild worked out a pattern compatible with that of the main windows but more closely resembling traditional geometric arabesques. This design, executed on some parts of the screen in positive pattern and on others in negative, was amber-stained on three-quarter-inch-thick float glass by Kitsilano Stained Glass of Vancouver. The float glass was used here for its transparency, so as to preserve a view of the beautiful Islamic-style garden outside.

When we arrived at the mosque, we first noticed the landscaped courtyard surrounded by trees and a high cast-concrete wall. The attention to detail in every aspect of the mosque and its environs was apparent as we passed through the beautifully crafted, handmade, steel courtyard gates. The mosque itself is a striking monolithic edifice on whose outside surface is a beautiful interplay of shapes contrasted in cast concrete and Carrara sandstone. The clean, quiet stateliness of the building from without is ample evidence in itself of the dedication of the architect to his project. From certain perspectives the intriguing three-dimensional main windows (*See* Plate 23) are visible, surrounded by a wide border of smooth concrete that showcases them in the sandstone walls.

Approaching the marble-faced entranceway at the front end of the mosque and passing through the brass-inlaid, carved hardwood doors into the foyer, the visitor's first glimpse of the interior's ground floor is of the area reserved for religious functions, which lies just beyond a carved wood screen. The prayer area is truly grand. With its three-dimensional ceiling of deep-coffered recesses and octagonal domes, its wall accentuated by stained-glass, inlaid oak filigree screens, and marmorina (cast marble dust) tiles, and its carpets whose octagonal designs are woven in relief into the deep pile, it communicates the over-all impression that one has passed into a special realm — an Islamic world. In that hushed, ordered, finely wrought environment, we were enveloped by an atmosphere of deep composure.

Since it was afternoon, the windows were the main sources of light in the mosque's ground floor, and the light passing through them was softened by the opalescent glass and warmed by the translucent silver stain with which the windows were adorned. At the same time the glass's opalescence completed the process of separating us from the outside world. In terms of both their shape and their stained pattern (*See* Plate 24), the windows seemed integrated with the over-all design. Simplicity was the key to their success. Given the plenitude of the building's ornamentation, what was called for in the windows was subtlety.

"It's very difficult to reduce everything to its absolute minimum," Haufschild says. "The thing that I like about my work in the mosque is that it is very restrained."

Whether an individual design is bold or restrained, Haufschild strives for what is appropriate. When asked about the inspiration for his artistic ideas, he cites the reading he does and the people he knows in the worlds of art and architecture. It is evident, too, that he continues to be very much the globe-crossing participant/observer. "One of the things that I'm most excited about is the continual learning process," he says. "I'm learning more now than when I went to school—because I'm using, in practical ways, what I learn."

It seems very likely that Canada's public places will continue to benefit from the results of Lutz Haufschild's learning process for many years to come. The future of stained glass in Canada is in the hands of the architects and developers, Haufschild feels, as long as glass artists know how to work and how to present their ideas. He predicts big things for the country: "Canada, per capita, has more high-caliber architects than most countries. As long as there are glass artists of the same caliber, the future of stained glass in Canada is secure."

PLATE 23: (Left) Burnaby Jamatkhana, 1984. View of one of 8 main windows as seen from the outside; each 8 × 14 sq. ft. (2.44 × 4.27 m) Burnaby, B.C. J.R.

PLATE 24: (Right) Burnaby Jamatkhana, 1984. View of one of 8 main windows as seen from the inside; each 8 × 14 sq. ft. (2.44 × 4.27 m) Burnaby, B.C. L.H.

Sarah Hall

In the early 1960s, when Sarah Hall was about ten, her father was the chairman of a church committee charged with the responsibility for overseeing the design of a new church building. He took her with him on a tour of churches, during which she often had to sit patiently in the pews and wait. She became fascinated with the stained glass that she saw in these buildings. It was not long before she decided that what she wanted to do in life was to design stained glass.

That youthful aspiration abided through the years. However, as Hall reached the age where she might actually pursue this interest, she found that there were not many opportunities for apprenticeship in Canada. In the mid-seventies she studied for a year at Sheridan College's School of Crafts and Design, taking courses in painting, photography, and art history, as well as stained glass. Feeling that there were few possibilities for learning more about stained glass in Canada, she enrolled in 1975 at the Swansea College of Art, in Wales, where she would study under the renowned Lawrence Lee (who designed some of the stained glass in the rebuilt Coventry Cathedral). Here at Swansea she continued to study art history and went on fascinating tours of medieval churches. During 1976–77, after her studies at Swansea, she stayed in Britain as an apprentice to Lawrence Lee, who was working in a studio in Kent. Hall's assiduous efforts ultimately resulted in a diploma in Architectural Stained Glass from the Guilds of London Institute.

While in Europe, Hall traveled to see numerous examples of historical and modern stained glass, including the work of the great contemporary German artists. She found the work of Georg Meistermann, in particular, very interesting. During 1977–78, Hall spent time in Israel doing a photographic study of Middle Eastern glass and mosaics. Upon returning to Canada, she worked for part of 1978 as an assistant to stained-glass artist Stephen Taylor, who ran a studio in Toronto at the time.

When Hall set up her own studio in Toronto in 1979, she was a well-traveled, well-trained artist ready to begin her own very personal path of exploration in the medium. In a very short time she began to receive commissions for residential work.

The interior French doors that Hall designed for the Kelley residence in Richmond Hill, Ontario (*See* Plate 25), offer an example of her good judgment in designing architecturally integrated work. Hall was actually commissioned to design the wooden doors themselves, as well as the stained glass they frame; she gave the ensemble the title *Sea/Sky*. To insure that the windows would look good in both reflected and transmitted light, she chose to use a lot of semi-opaque glass and a much smaller proportion of transparent glass. Over-all, the windows' composition is symmetrical. The artist derived the hexagonal shape featured in the upper portion of the windows from the parquetry pattern in the hardwood floor, furthering the integration of the doors with the house's interior. Hall used moderate color in the water motif at the bottom of the windows and the sky motif at the top. She exercised admirable restraint in leaving large areas in the middle of each door panel blank; in some settings simplicity can be desirable.

Hall does not feel that the design for a window need always be strictly determined by the architecture of the place where it will be installed. "Sometimes you want a piece to fit in with the architecture so that your work becomes an extension of it, and at other times you may want the work to be a counterpoint. You don't always have to reflect the building

PLATE 25: (Left) *Sea/Sky*, Kelley residence, 1981. Interior doors, each panel 15 × 60 in. (38.1 × 152.4 cm) Richmond Hill, Ontario.

PLATE 26: (Right) *Conception*, Kelley residence, 1981. 47 × 49 in. (119.4 × 124.5 cm) Richmond Hill, Ontario.

in the window." This contradicts a tenet commonly held in stained-glass circles. But, clearly, Hall is not one to shrink from heresy.

"When I initially look at a client's home, I go there with the client and spend quite a while there," she says. "And what I'm looking for is what the light is like. I talk to the client about what kind of mood they want to create, because I think light is very powerful in that way. The window has to be right for that room, and that person, and the activities that will take place there. I find bringing all of those things together really exciting."

In designing with recognizable forms, natural imagery, and a generous use of organic line, Hall bucks current Canadian stained-glass trends. "There is certainly peer pressure to steer away from natural forms," she admits. "But I really feel that it's the way I should be working, so I have to go that way. There's a real fascination with using the images of technology in art right now. But I think it's impersonal, and I don't like it." Although a good deal of amateurish or banal design is done using natural imagery, Sarah Hall's work proves that an artist can work with such imagery in a manner that's both fresh and sophisticated.

The window, titled *Conception*, that sits above the stairwell of the Kelley residence in Richmond Hill (*See* Plate 26) is an interesting work. It provides light for the stairwell and for the house's second floor. The window's delicate, subtly complex design blends organic and geometric elements, the focal image being a nautilus shell in cross-section. To delineate the chambers of the shell, Hall utilized the acid-etching technique quite expertly, eroding away some of the colored surface of the blue flashed glass that she used. The manner in which she has interwoven the shell form with the background and the colored horizontal bands is quite intriguing. Vitually all the colors in the window are in the green-blue-purple range, giving the window a soothing quality difficult to obtain with a greater variety of hues. The use of transparent glass allows the window to pass a considerable amount of light.

Hall's accomplishment in acid etching is praised by other stained-glass workers. In fact, she is experienced with quite a range of glass-working techniques, including silver staining, sandblasting, and *dalle de verre*. "I find the exploration of technical frontiers provides quite a challenge," she says. "I think any technique that you want to use is fair enough. What you want to *say* is the important thing."

Of course, what is "said" is said visually; any attempt to translate that into verbal terms can meet with only limited success. It is this matter of saying something visually that is the chief aim of stained-glass artists who, like Sarah Hall, take an intimate, extremely personal approach to glass design. And in order to "say" meaningful things in new ways, it is important to understand what has been said in the art of the past. Hall has seen a lot of historical and contemporary stained glass in Europe and North America at firsthand, and she has also studied the available literature in considerable depth. She is especially interested in European stained glass dating from the twelfth to the fifteenth centuries. But like many serious stained-glass artists, she has a keen interest in artistic media besides glass. She named English religious and landscape painter Stanley Spencer as one of her favorite artists, along with Munch, Klee, Modigliani, Chagall, and the color-field painter Barnett Newman.

All of this amounts to a background Hall can draw upon in her own work. Even so, each commission is its own challenge. "When I first start designing a piece, I have a difficult time getting down to it. I spend about two weeks pacing," Hall jokes. She often does a lot of research, including looking at books of paintings for stimulation. But inspiration often comes from non-visual sources, as well. "I'll be reading and I'll start seeing a lot of mental pictures," Hall says. The forms of the natural world constitute a reservoir of images for her to draw on in the challenging process of designing. "Finally, once I get settled into the work, the design takes anywhere from a couple of days to a couple of weeks. Sometimes I have to get onto a new track if something really isn't working."

Hall sees sketching as an intrinsically valuable activity that can feed into the design process indirectly. Because of the central importance of sketching in the design process, Hall feels that the artist who cannot draw well is sadly limited in the ability to design. Consequently, she devotes time to sketching outside of the process of preparing a piece, as well as within it.

In the window she designed for the 1984 Koffler Gallery stained-glass exhibition (See Plate 27), Hall contemplated the biblical Exodus story that explores a theme of freedom versus restriction; the theme was prompted by the fact that the gallery is located in Toronto's Jewish Community Centre, and that the exhibition coincided with Passover. Titled *Towards Canaan*, the window pits graceful organic shapes against a simple geometric structure. Hall did a lot of background research for this design and brought in an Egyptian reference; the contrasting horizontal stripes, on either side of the outer vertical elements, bear some resemblance to the famous headdress on the beaten gold mask of Tutankhamen's coffin. While shapes resembling clouds, or even birds in flight, seem to be escaping from the geometric frame, the structure is still essentially intact. It seems that, for Hall, the symbolism has a general philosophical meaning. "I don't know that I believe in absolute freedom," she comments. She used a variety of different glasses in the window, which was assembled with

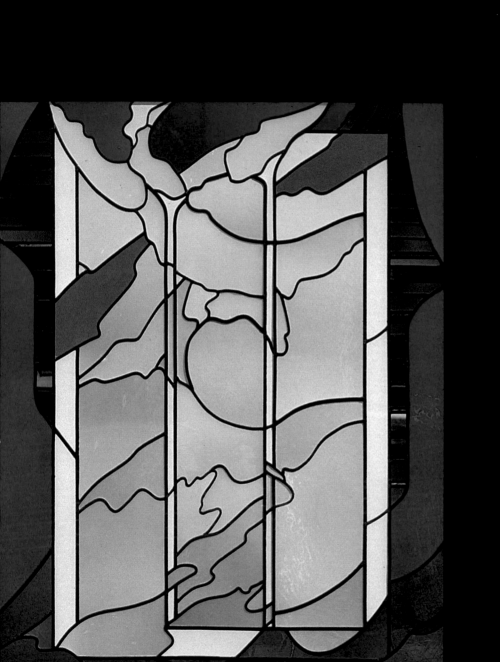

standard leading technique. Her tasteful restraint in color gives this piece a strong but tempered feeling. Appropriately enough, the panel was bought by a man working toward a Ph.D. in theology, and is now installed as a window in his home.

In its graphic quality, Hall's work seems thoroughly North American. Yet, because of the years she spent studying in Britain and traveling in Europe, her sense of connection with the world of contemporary stained glass is vividly international. Besides the artists whom she knows and sees from time to time in Canada, she keeps in touch with some whom she knows from her art-school days in England. This background, coupled with the fact that she has done a little teaching, has given her an interesting perspective on how novices approach the medium here, now that training opportunities have expanded somewhat, as opposed to how they approach it in Europe. "The students here have no preconceptions — they'll try anything! And sometimes it works. There's a kind of lightness here that Europe will never be able to equal because of its thousand-year tradition. I love tradition, but there is something about North America that I find lighter, more adventurous, and exciting."

Though Hall is well aware of the pitfalls of the recent enormous growth of popularity of stained glass as a hobby in Canada, she is quick to point out that it has meant that supplies are much more readily available than they were a decade ago when her serious interest was just unfolding.

There is something in a genuine artist besides knowledge of the materials and processes of the medium, besides even technical accomplishment, that separates him or her from the dilettante. Is that "something more" an earnestness, or, perhaps, a sense of commitment to an adventure? It is hard to say. Asked why stained glass continues to engage her, Hall replies, "There is a lot for me to explore. For me, it's all a process, you feel very open, and when you close up, you know itself. When I look at a finished piece, I see aspects where I didn't take a risk." And what comprises the audience before which the artist takes those risks? Clients? Fellow artists? "Most importantly it's myself. At certain points in a creative process, you feel very open, and when you close up, you know it. To me it's a matter of whether I've pushed myself as far as I can go."

PLATE 27: *Towards Canaan,* Bosworth residence, 1984. 37 × 53 in. (94 × 134.6 cm) Toronto, Ontario.

J.R.

Brenda Malkinson

In the mid-1970s Brenda Malkinson was working at the Alberta Provincial Museum, in Edmonton, as an exhibition designer. She was a bit bored with the job, so she took on some freelance book and magazine illustration work on the side. The illustration jobs established her reputation as a capable designer, and led to her being offered the opportunity to design stained-glass windows for a church, if she cared to try her hand at this medium. She was intrigued with the idea and set out to learn the basic techniques of stained-glass construction by consulting some artisans at a local, commercial stained-glass studio. The windows she designed ultimately turned out so well that the craftspeople at this glass studio asked Malkinson if she would like to do some designing for them. She followed up this offer, accepting, in lieu of cash payment, lessons in stained-glass construction technique.

A while later, as fate would have it, Malkinson was a patron in a restaurant that was to be renovated. Hearing that the proprietors wanted a stained-glass window made, she informed them that she could do the job. She sold them the window for the cost of the materials alone, but its installation, in turn, led to a commission for a residential window. It did not take Malkinson long to see the career potential in what she had stumbled into, and she soon adopted a more businesslike approach to working in stained glass. She has been a full-time professional glass artist since 1976.

As an exhibition designer, Malkinson had an art background. She had taken a four-year illustration curriculum at Alberta College of Art in Calgary. After that she spent a year in London, England, studying theater-set and costume design at the Central School of Art. "There was a major stained-glass department there," Malkinson relates, "and I came back to Canada with lots of photographs."

Malkinson's natural artistic ability was fostered by her years of commercial-art and theater-design training. But as a stained-glass artist, she is essentially self-taught. "I look at what I've done on my own as my 'training,' really," she says. "I can learn easily from books, and I do a lot of reading. I feel pretty good about having done it myself. I think it kept me from being too stiff, in many ways. There are probably some things I could have learned a little quicker. But I've always maintained that if you like something well enough, you'll learn how to do it really well no matter *how* you learn it."

Never having been dominated by any one approach to design, Malkinson sees herself as a natural observer, an absorber of influences. "I'm constantly at the library, looking at what's current in the art journals," she says. "As far as stained glass goes, there may be a particular influence from the German designers, because they've gotten a lot of exposure in publications we can get in Canada. I wouldn't say I've been very deliberate in my study of historical glass. I've paid more attention to contemporary work."

Malkinson's early work consisted mostly of fairly literal representations of the natural world—finely wrought pieces based on strong, straightforward designs. One such piece was incorporated into the Massey Foundation Collection of contemporary Canadian craft, and featured in the book *The Craftsman's Way*. Her more recent works, however, have been either abstractions of observable things or thoroughly abstract embodiments of feelings. While her windows and independent panels usually have an immediate visual appeal, her purposes extend beyond mere graphic novelty. "I have to go deeper than visual effect," she says. "I want painting, sculpture, or glass to give me an emotional impact. For me, it's like a frozen river, where I know that water is running

PLATE 28: (Below, left) Royal
Alexander Hospital Chapel,
1983. 4 panels, each 18 × 96 in.
(45.7 × 243.8 cm) Edmonton,
Alberta.

PLATE 29: (Below, right)
Water Spirits, Beans and Barley
Restaurant, 1981. 3 panels, each
4 × 6 ft. (1.22 × 1.83 m)
Edmonton, Alberta.

J.R.

L.D.

BRENDA MALKINSON 111

underneath, and life exists under the frozen surface. There are depths of human nature that we have no words for. Visual art should look beyond the surface of reality."

The windows that Malkinson designed for the new chapel at Edmonton's Royal Alexandra Hospital (*See* Plate 28) are beautifully appropriate to both the architecture and the function of the room. Their rectangles of color, quietly interrupted by organic shapes, add a tranquil accent to the chapel's exterior wall, contrasting nicely with the plate-glass windows with their vertical blinds and wooden latticework screens. After Malkinson was approached by the architects who had designed the chapel, she got her bearings for the design process through consultation with the hospital's chaplain, who wanted a spiritually meaningful but non-sectarian design.

The artist explained her design to us as we viewed the windows: "I was thinking about why people go to hospitals, and at the time I was reading a book about human separation. Basically, the two large purple rectangles in each of the four windows represent human beings. There are two because they represent the separation of someone from their family or friends, or the separation of mother and child at birth, or the separation of a death. The lines that run through the bottom rectangles are like the bloodstream, and the lines that come down from the top of the windows are the divine life force — whatever a person may call it. The windows are meant to have a flowing feeling, to give a sense of well-being. The colors are red, purple, and blue — the colors that most religions consider to be sacred." We felt that the windows contributed considerably to the comforting calm of the chapel.

Malkinson designed her three panels, titled *Water Spirits* (*See* Plate 29), to harmonize with the primeval keynote of the interior-design theme. Made with German and French antique glasses, the panels are artificially backlit. They appear to be three frames capturing a sequence of moments in some continuously mobile, fluid process. The smooth, surging forms in vivid blue, red, and white are captivating. The artist told us that the design's conception derived from sketches made while she was hiking in the Rockies. The design of these windows seems typical of Malkinson's work, which tends toward a certain mildness and joyous integration.

"The individuality in my art comes from my passion for freedom and immediacy at that point where my skill becomes unconscious and my mind concentrates completely on what it wants to say," says Malkinson. "I want to always maintain a capacity for discovery and self-renewal."

Malkinson's primary focus in stained glass is architectural work, but she has done quite a number of independent panels. Her diptych *Soaring* (*See* Plates 30 and 31) presents a good example of her more recent, abstract work. The panels were commissioned for the Universiade Games World Craft Exhibition in Edmonton. "They're about soaring," Malkinson says. "At the time I designed them, I was doing a lot of flying in a glider, with a friend. I didn't want to portray the theme in a literal way, I wanted to capture the *feeling* of soaring. I used etching in the top portions to bring in the swirling sense of clouds. When you're soaring, you get breaks in the clouds where you see the landscape, but it's not necessarily as you see it on the ground, where you have horizon lines; it's often straight in front of you or to the right of you. There's no ordinary vantage point." The panels, then, bring in elements of an actual experience, and the elements of objective reality have been transformed by the artist's subjective reactions to the sensations of soaring.

The composition of the pieces in the *Soaring* diptych is

PLATE 30: *Soaring*, diptych
(left panel), 1983. Each panel
24 × 48 in. (61 × 121.9 cm)
Collection of C. Zwarych.

114 BRENDA MALKINSON

PLATE 31: *Soaring*, diptych
(right panel), 1983. Each panel,
24 × 48 in. (61 × 121.9 cm)
Collection of C. Zwarych.

BRENDA MALKINSON 115

quite a bit looser than that in much of Malkinson's other work. Except for the two straight vertical lines in the top of each panel that function as a sort of border, the lines waver. Combined with the strong colors (red, yellow, and purple), this gives the diptych a blithe, nonchalant quality. It is interesting that the artist used the acid-etching technique, rather than sandblasting, to obtain the frosted "cloud" effect in the upper portion of each panel.

"Work is a statement about yourself," Malkinson comments. "In the autonomous work I try to let the statement really come out. In commissioned work, your clients want you to convey some particular feeling, so that has to be there. Even then you can't help but put a piece of *you* in there."

In 1981 Malkinson designed and made three panels for the Beans and Barley restaurant in Edmonton. As part of its décor the restaurant was to have several pools of water and an artificial waterfall, all intended to create an interesting, peaceful atmosphere.

Like a number of other artists we spoke to, Malkinson maintains that opportunities for discovery and self-renewal arise in all aspects of life, not only in the artist's practice of art. She finds that the creative work of others frequently stimulates her own ideas. She enjoys live theater and says that she often finds herself watching a play through squinted eyes, in order to reduce the stage production to a set of mobilrelationships in form and color. She plays piano, and finds, from her understanding of musical structure, consistent inspiration in music. Her tastes run to the classics and the work of certain contemporary composer-instrumentalists. Useful visual images often come to her while reading, and she enjoys a wide range of literature; she mentions in particular such disparate writers as Leonard Cohen and C. G. Jung. Malkinson always keeps a sketchbook nearby so that images that form in her mind can be recorded and worked out on paper.

While much of Malkinson's recent work has been fabricated using the traditional leaded technique, she has also used copper-foil construction extensively. Her use of etching, painting, laminating, and slumping in some pieces indicates a tendency in her current work. "The direction that I want to go in with these new techniques is more of a sculptural, dimensional one — more getting rid of the leadline. Being a painter at heart, these lines are starting to bother me. I'm trying to get more of a 'flow' happening, more tonation of color. I'm trying to manipulate the glass more.

"At this point, people can usually pick my work out of the crowd, so I guess I have a style," Malkinson continues. "But I'm growing and changing. I don't think you ever have to stop growing."

When asked what made her stay with glass as her chief medium of expression, she thinks for a while, then replies: "I find glass an exciting medium that gives me a greater satisfaction than other media I'm involved with. To me, seeing the quality of light changing within the glass is like sensing the strong emotion contained within a slow dance."

Barbara Laffey

JOEL RUSS

Some years ago Barbara Laffey acquired an old house with a number of broken stained-glass windows in it. She decided she would like to learn the skills needed to fix the windows herself. Laffey happened to live around the corner from a stained-glass supply store, so she bought some tools and a how-to book there and began to teach herself what she would need to know. As she proceeded in her repair project, her interest grew along with her skill. She decided to make a stained-glass window from scratch for the bathroom in the house, and this turned out to be only the first of several that she made for her home. Impressed by the window they saw in her bathroom, friends began to ask her about the possibility of her doing work for them.

During this time Laffey became friends with the woman who owned the nearby stained-glass shop, Mimi Gellman, whose design work Laffey admired. After a while Laffey and Gellman decided to form a partnership in the stained-glass business; it seemed like a good idea because Laffey could bring her background in management into the enterprise, while Mimi Gellman could contribute technical and artistic understanding of the medium. Their intention was to sell anything and everything that could be made in stained glass: windows, hanging panels, lampshades, and so on.

At this point in her life, Laffey had a varied background related to the arts and to the business end of creative pursuits. Born in Chicago, Laffey had been the kind of child who wondered what she could *make* on rainy days, rather than what was on TV. During her university years, beginning in the late sixties, prior to her immigration to Canada, she began taking art courses at the University of Illinois. Laffey's university stretches were interrupted by time taken off from school for work. In one of these between-enrollment periods she worked in the film department of Columbia College. One of the perquisites of working there was the opportunity to take, tuition-free, any courses she wanted. In the free time she had available, she took advantage of the opportunity to study printmaking and film animation, and to take several other film-related courses.

Laffey moved to Toronto in 1971, where she enrolled for a year in the Ontario College of Art. "That was a year when they were going through a lot of political upheaval in the school," Laffey relates. "The Conceptualists were battling with the Abstractionists and the Traditionalists, and it was wonderful! So I went there full-time, with no expectations and no intentions. I took traditional life-drawing classes and some pretty non-traditional courses. A lot of what I did there was conceptual work. I also did some mixed-media sculptural work." After her year at the College of Art, Laffey kept her hand in with night-school courses in such varied areas as art history and cartooning. Her business sense developed through the variety of production positions she held with publishers and advertising agencies, and particularly through the six years she spent working in the Canadian feature-film industry as a production manager responsible at times for multi-million-dollar budgets. All of this prepared her excellently for running a commercial stained-glass business.

Laffey told us about her years in partnership with Mimi Gellman: "I came to the business with formal design training, no professional glass experience whatsoever, and a good business sense. We taught each other. Mimi was such a perfectionist in crafting windows that I learned to be a perfectionist, too. In the first year, she did the lion's share of the designing. After a while, when the business was functioning normally, we both did design and fabrication. We'd help each other in fabricating each other's panels, but basically I designed my work and made it, and she designed her work and made it."

Shortly after opening the studio, Laffey attended a slide lecture on German stained glass given by Lutz Haufschild. Realizing that she had no real idea of the current potential of stained glass, she began to make a concerted study of contemporary glass through books and journals.

Laffey left her partnership with Gellman as a result of a personal crisis. She spent part of 1983 in the hospital with a life-threatening illness and decided, as a result, to take a non-commercial direction with her stained glass. "I just made a decision that I wasn't going to do something that didn't mean something to me anymore. I wasn't going to do something just for money, because all my life I had made job compromises and had gone and worked for the money. It becomes really difficult to create something just for the money once you've set yourself a standard. That was the moving force behind the closing of the studio." Gellman supported Laffey's decision. The split of the partnership made it possible for both of them to pursue careers in stained-glass-as-art.

Having decided to take stained glass seriously, Laffey has sought to expand her understanding by studying with master glass designers. She has participated in several workshops with Jochem Poensgen — in Toronto, at the Pilchuck School of Glass in Washington State, and in West Germany. She has also studied briefly with Johannes Schreiter and American architect/glass-designer Kenneth vonRoenn.

The direction Laffey's new, non-commercial work began to take can be seen in the free-standing piece (*See* Plate 32) she made in 1983, when she was invited to participate in a show at the Ontario Crafts Council Gallery. Titled "About

Space," the exhibition featured pieces that explored three-dimensionality. Laffey designed an elegant room-dividing screen that stands six feet high and four and one-half feet wide; two of the five separate panels that make up the screen stand in a vertical plane seven inches from that of the other three.

The piece offered the opportunity for several veins of exploration. One of these was the aspect of limited three-dimensionality, which brought a kinetic element into the screen. "I was interested in the effect of movement when you walk past the piece. The front plane appears to move across the back plane," Laffey says. "And I like the fact that it changes wherever you sit in the room, even though it's very geometric. Some of the gestural lines align with those behind them, and some don't, and that was quite deliberate. I made pen-and-ink scribbles on acctate and used them as collage elements in designing the piece; then I transferred them to lead. Actually, this is the first piece I made with a sandblasted background grid."

With its predominance of light-toned transparent yellow glass, its subtle sandblasted background grid, and its almost calligraphic lead overlay lines sailing across the glass, the piece lends a warm, breezy feeling to a room.

Laffey's use of the lead overlays in this piece represents her desire not to confine drawing to the design process, but to bring it into the finished work. "A lot of the main concepts in my work right now have to do with contrast, and with the hand. It seems that a lot of the designs I've been working on lately have been quite geometric. But there's a part of me that comes out of my life-drawing experience that wants to just put a squiggle, a line, a paint stroke over the geometry, and integrate the two."

PLATE 32: Room dividing screen, 1983. 4.5 ft. wide × 6 ft. high × 7 in. deep (1.37 m wide × 1.83 m high × 17.8 cm deep) Private collection.

When we interviewed her, Laffey's current direction of development involved eliminating the leadline by applying various pigments directly to plate glass. This method is reminiscent of the glass-as-transparent-canvas approach developed in Europe in the fifteenth and sixteenth centuries. But the materials Laffey uses are thoroughly up-to-date. She has been doing some real ground-breaking work in developing her new techniques.

In 1984 Laffey began exploring these new methods in independent panels. Her first opportunity to apply them to an architectural situation came later that year with a commission to design four sixteen-by-sixty-inch windows (*See* Plate 33) for the living room of a Toronto residence. The client mistrusted geometric design because she wanted to avoid a

visual effect that might be too harsh. At the same time, Laffey was leaning toward an approach that would bring more spontaneity and more evidence of her hand into her designs. She developed two designs for the residence's windows: a reasonably conventional one, incorporating glass bevels, and an unorthodox one that would involve layers of airy, gestural linework (a reference to the client's involvement with weaving) painted directly onto glass. Although both design approaches appealed to the client, she chose the painted glass design for the simple — and laudable — reason that it was riskier. The risk was actually twofold. There was an esthetic risk in that the windows would not resemble conventional stained glass. But a risk at least as great was that Laffey was still working out the techniques required to execute such conceptions.

"One important consideration in the design of these windows was that they be enjoyable at night, as well as in the daytime," Laffey explains. "So much traditional glass work turns black at night, and since the client entertains at home in the evening, it was important to overcome this problem. The reflective-coated, bronze-colored glass I chose as a background — and the use of liquid gold, which is also reflective — provided materials which transformed themselves with changing light conditions." In other words, the windows' translucent qualities dominate in the daytime, while their reflective qualities come into play in the evening. Each window is actually a composite of four sandwiched layers of glass — one is the bronze reflective glass; the other three each bear some aspect of the design, which is painted on with enamels, silver stain, and liquid gold, respectively. This liquid gold, by the way, is a fluid suspension of actual gold.

"In order to fabricate the windows, I had to find an industrial furnace that would heat the glass to a high enough temperature to fire the enamels, silver stain, and gold on, without leaving marks on the glass," Laffey explains. "I found such a furnace at Inkan [Ltd.], one designed for the tempering of glass. I then had to work closely with industrial chemists on the formulation of gold, silver stain, and enamels that would withstand the high firing temperature and short firing time, and still give the desired results. It took many months of experimentation, lots of trial and error, before we came up with formulas that worked dependably."

The ultimate result of these efforts pleased the artist, the client, and the people at the industrial firms who assisted Laffey in the processes involved. Because of the airy, abstract approach Laffey took with the design of these windows, she managed to avoid the universally disparaged effects of the glass painting practiced during the sixteenth through nineteenth centuries, when, with lamentable results, glass artists were emulating, on glass, the approach of the oil painter.

As with this residential commission, Laffey now tends to approach the independent panel as a field for experimentation, rather than an end in itself. She expresses a strong preference for designing architectural glass. "I rarely do autonomous work," she says. "Most of my work is commissioned. I've felt like a kite without a string — one that won't fly — when I haven't had the givens of an architectural situation: this window, this space, this light, these people living there."

Whatever technical direction Barbara Laffey's work may take in the future, her initiative and commitment to artistic integrity promise to make her evolution in glass design worth watching.

PLATE 33: (Overleaf) Private residence, 1984. 4 windows, each 16 × 60 in. (40.6 × 152.4 cm) Toronto, Ontario. *Photograph by Barbara Laffey.*

Gundar Robez

Gundar Robez makes no bones about his belief in the independent stained-glass panel. Probably he doesn't need to, because the appeal of his dynamic, venturous panels has been remarkably wide. Over the last decade, he has produced many fine pieces that have ultimately been displayed by his patrons as *objets d'art*, much as paintings are.

Besides the fact that most, though not all, of Robez's *oeuvre* consists of panels without architectural reference, many of his works have the look of paintings. Yet in general Robez has used the standard, contemporary, leaded-glass approach to fabrication, in which the color is provided solely by pieces of cut glass. Because Robez does not achieve his effect by actually painting on the glass, the painterly appearance of his work is all the more remarkable. It stems primarily from the immediacy and motion of his designs.

While Robez's designs are not bound by any one school or style of modern art, certain influences have obviously contributed to their painterly quality, influences the artist readily discusses. "While I was in school I was taking influence from all sorts of sources," he says. "But later I never looked to glass artists for inspiration. I enjoy other people's glass work, and I like to see what's going on; but for inspiration I've turned to painters: the Expressionists and Impressionists up through people like Klee and Kandinsky. Also the Abstract Expressionists of the fifties, though no one artist in particular. My favorites change over time."

The design of panels like *Pomp and Be Bop* and *Elation #4* bear an obvious yet deceptive resemblance to some of the loosely painted, passionately expressive works of such Action Painters as Jackson Pollock, Willem de Kooning, and Franz Kline. Certainly, while he is working out a design, there is much similarity between Robez's approach and the approaches

JOEL RUSS

of some of the Action Painters. But beneath an untrammeled surface similar to Abstract Expressionism in its dynamism of gesture lies a more disciplined control of effect necessitated by the glass panel's material. Because of the several technical stages involved in transferring a design conception to glass, much of the effort of actualizing a panel goes into the execution of a composition decided upon early in the process. This is in sharp contrast to the Action Painters' approach—unpremeditated and instinctive from beginning to end—wherein color might be applied layer upon layer.

Robez says that when designing he usually does a number of sketches, sometimes on the same theme, and sometimes not. When exhausted by a sketching session, he leaves a design alone until the next day, at which time he comes back and fine-tunes it. "I'm fairly orderly about construction," he comments. "Once I've established something on paper, I tend to follow it pretty closely. But color in glass is a quantum leap from color on paper. If there's to be any spontaneity after establishing the design, it usually comes in when choosing the glass." Spontaneity, then, is mostly confined to his design process. His skill in fabrication allows him the great freedom of design that his panels display.

Formal labels aside, most of Robez's work is both abstract and expressionistic. The relatively small proportion of his work that is figurative is still expressionistic in its transformation of recognizable forms according to the dictates of the artist's feelings. But Robez's expressive manner varies. Some of his pieces are much more lyrical than would be suggested by any association with Abstract Expressionism. *Outer Space*, with its broad strokes of color and its incessantly fluid motion, is reminiscent of some of the very interesting—though difficult to categorize—work done in the late sixties and early

PLATE 34: *Pomp and Be Bop,*
1982. 85 × 48 in. (215.9 ×
121.9 cm) Collection of artist.

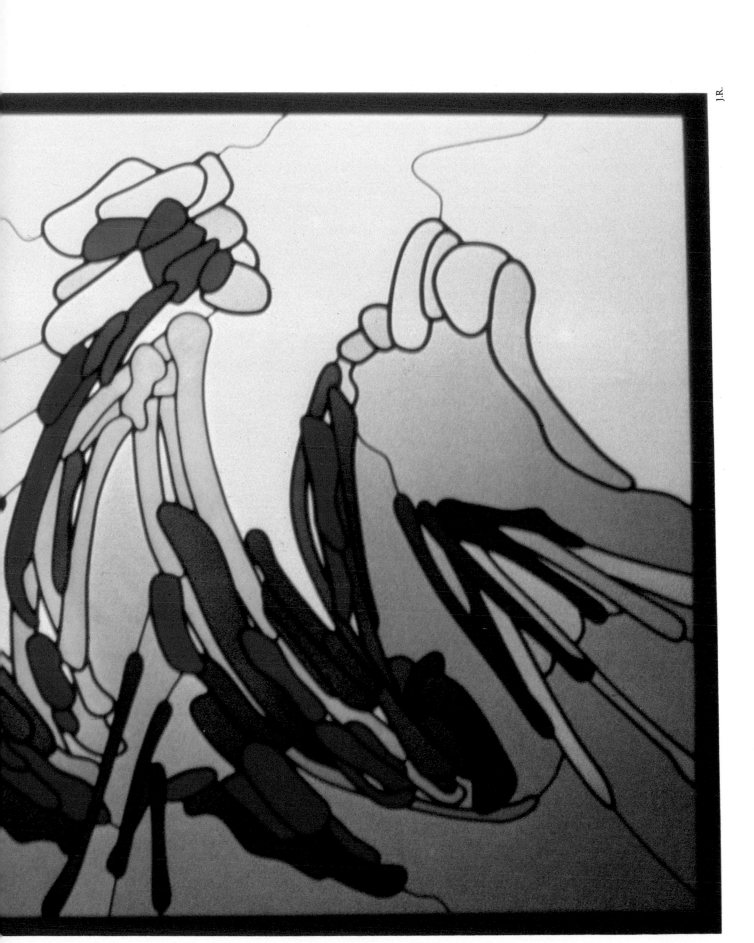

seventies by East Coast American painter Arlene Sklar-Weinstein.

One might expect that Gundar Robez was trained as a painter, yet this is not so. In the early 1970s he commenced studies at Sheridan College's School of Crafts and Design, starting out with the intention of learning to make jewelry. However, the curriculum included training in the rudiments of a number of disciplines, among them hot-glass work. Robez was soon seduced away from jewelry by glass. "I found the process of making jewelry tedious, whereas with glass — especially hot glass — the process itself was very spontaneous; the action was immediately on the end of the blowpipe." He soon reorganized his course of study to revolve around glass sculpture.

During Robez's last year at Sheridan, Robert Jekyll, who was teaching there at the time, introduced him to stained glass. Robez recalls how he discovered his natural artistic strengths — and weaknesses — as they related to stained glass: "I discovered that I was a natural colorist. My lines, my forms, my compositions — I had to *work* on all of those. But, fortunately when you're working with stained glass, you're working with the purest form of color."

Robez graduated from Sheridan with a degree in glass sculpture in 1976. That year he also set up a glass studio in Hamilton equipped to cold-work glass. He started to design and fabricate his very personal statements in stained glass, within a short while selling the first piece he produced at a professional exhibition.

Though Robez admits to having little interest in historical glass, he is well versed in the contemporary glass scenes in North America and Europe; indeed, he is something of an authority on the Canadian scene and has lectured on the subject. He has studied briefly with Lawrence Lee, Johannes Schreiter, and Jochem Poensgen, though he feels these European masters have had little direct influence on his work.

Robez has always done his own fabrication and has continued to develop his technical repertoire since his graduation from Sheridan. "I believe in the intrinsic beauty of glass itself; but anything goes — technique is wide open, as far as I'm concerned. I will use traditional techniques, but I have no reservations about experimenting." Robez is fully confident with virtually any type of glass-working process, and although he has often used such surface treatments as sandblasting and acid etching, many of his most exciting pieces have been made with the most common techniques — which he uses with remarkable facility. Indeed, his skill with a glass cutter, that most basic of glass-working tools, impresses seasoned artisans; and without this finesse many of his panels would lose a considerable amount of their suppleness and verve.

Robez's 1982 piece, *Pomp and Be Bop* (*See* Plate 34), with its intricately shaped pieces, is a good example of this. It is a dancing visual frolic of colorful, wavelike forms, one following the other. Its mood is utterly joyful. It was inspired by music, as the title suggests. Robez had been listening to a lot of jazz around the time he got the idea for the panel; but, while he was designing, his contemplations turned to older forms of music. "I was thinking about musical structure and what it means. When I think of structure, I usually associate it with the classics. But jazz *has* structure, though it's an underlying thing." Once he had sketched out the rhythmic main elements of the design, he was reminded of a procession or parade, and the title of Elgar's familiar series of marches, "Pomp and Circumstance," came to mind. But, of course, Robez's piece embodies a good deal more vigor and playfulness than Elgar's — thus the "Be Bop."

Each of the leaping "waves" in this striking design is unique in its makeup, though each decidedly participates in the overall rhythm. Looking closely, one notices the brisk shapes of the myriad component glass pieces that make up the design. Robez chose to set the colorful foreground elements against a two-level background, an upper portion of semi-opaque white glass, and a lower of transparent lavender glass.

Glass artists frequently speak of how the coloration of their work has become more subdued as they have matured in their medium; but Robez's growth as an artist has not seemed to require him to abandon powerful color. In his work, he seeks to communicate emotionally with the viewer, and frequently the hues he uses are unmuted, though they may be combined in such a way as to create either more or less intense effects. "There are people who are afraid of color. I'm not one of them," he remarks. "Every color has its use, depending upon the effect you intend."

The panel Robez has titled *Elation #4* (*See* Plate 35), which is ensconced in the Janovskis residence, is displayed—as a painting would be — against a wall. It is suspended out a short distance from this wall, from which is reflected the light of three spotlights, which backlights the piece. Robez also designed the interior decor of the room in which the piece is displayed. Were the room not meticulously decorated to accept it, a powerful piece like this might tend to clash with other decorative features. But the room is reasonably simple in its furnishings, its colors are subdued, and thus the sole spectacular piece of art in it works.

Elation #4 has the energetic quality common to much of the artist's work, but it communicates something much less ordered than *Pomp and Be Bop*. The jubilant explosion of biotic shape and saturated hue seems to emanate from below the bottom border of the panel, slightly to the left of the midpoint, and this lends an element of mystery to the event. This piece is part of a series of works Robez describes as "a celebration of sorts — of life, of humanity, of our natural environment." The painterly quality of this particular design results from the fact that it was actually worked out as a painted sketch, then transferred (via a cartoon) to the glass.

Elation #2 (*See* Plate 36), from the same series, offers an example of Robez's work built into a room, in this case into a set of interior French doors. The doors are in the home of a Toronto art consultant. According to Robez, the house was being renovated in 1979, and his client wanted the glass in the doors to be a strong focal point when viewed from either room. The decor of both rooms are kept uncluttered. The walls of one—the library—are paneled in dark woods; those of the other — the living room — are an off-white.

The doors are situated near the middle of the wall's width. Robez's design, emanating from the line where the two doors meet, lends both the wall and the doors themselves a welcome asymmetrical, bias-oriented feature. Robez developed and adapted the design he used from a sketch that was originally done in 1977. The main, or foreground, elements were cut from deeply colored, transparent antique glass, while the background was made from milky white French opalescent glass. Viewed in one manner, this pair of panels has an

PLATE 35: (Right) *Elation #4*,
1982. 50 × 41 in. (127 ×
104.1 cm) Collection of
I. Janovskis.

PLATE 36: (Below) *Elation #2*,
Himel residence, 1979. Interior
doors, each panel 22 × 68 in.
(55.9 × 172.7 cm) Toronto,
Ontario.

eruptive quality similar to *Elation #4*. But the shapes in these panels (being a bit reminiscent of the leaves of tropical plants) can also seem more placid or vegetative, and thus they engender a somewhat quieter feeling.

Although some of the stained glass Robez designs is intended for specific settings, much of it is independent. When an artist designs an independent piece on speculation, he has no control over how the piece is lit. Yet the type of illumination a stained-glass work has can have a considerable effect on its appearance, and thus on what it communicates to the viewer. "When you're designing for a particular environment, you can design in terms of a specific light source," he acknowledges. "I feel that natural light, with its purity and changing moods, is the most dramatic and beautiful, and given the choice I prefer to work with it. But I'm not a purist, and I believe that stained glass can be lit effectively with artificial light." He reveals that some of the pieces he has designed on spec. were conceived with front (reflected) lighting in mind, rather than, or in addition to, artificial or natural backlighting; but this specificity doesn't always enter into his design considerations.

In Robez's independent panel *Outer Space* (*See* Plate 37), we again encounter the joyous momentum found so frequently in his work. But the nature of the activity this time is a gamboling flux moving through dimensions of space that appear, disappear, and metamorphose into one another. The over-all sense of expansiveness of this peculiarly rapturous flow is suggested by the general tendency of the darker hues to "settle" to the bottom, while lighter hues tend to "rise," and occasional vertical elements thrust upward. Robez has employed quite a number of colors in this work. In some areas he has carefully chosen specific pieces of glass with subtly graduated saturation to suggest smoothly swelling movement. "The 'outer' in *Outer Space* refers partly to the saturated colors on the outside of the TV-like shape being played against the same colors, in lighter tones, in the inner part," Robez explains. It should be noted that he has reinforced the over-all effect of the composition by outlining some of the lighter-toned, curved shapes with dark lines of varying thickness; these are executed in glass, rather than lead. Another agreeable and perfectly congruous touch is provided by the graceful intrusion of overlaid leadlines into some of the colored areas.

Robez's stained-glass work is usually both emphatic and very personal. He frequently succeeds in his aim to communicate with others emotionally, and he does so by plumbing his own emotions. At times in his work there seems to be a desire to express visually some experience of the transcendence of the self. *Outer Space* strikes us as an example of this transpersonal aspect of Robez's work.

The forms to be seen in Robez's stained glass are varied, probably as varied as the special qualities of each of the experiences that give these forms meaning to the artist. The origins of the graphic ideas with which Robez expresses his perceptions are varied. "Sometimes a design starts when I just sit down at a table with a blank piece of paper and stare long enough; eventually something comes out of that meditative blankness," he says. "Sometimes I'm overwhelmed with an emotion, and I have a sort of intuitive, direct response that's almost an automatic movement of my hand." Robez works out these ideas through a number of means: watercolors, collage, pencil sketches, "things thrown on the floor." He tends to revise until he feels he's got it right.

When asked about a possible dominant theme in his work, Robez comments: "There are a number of thematic directions my work has gone in. Some things are erotic. And there's been a recurring musical theme. Lately I've been working with the design idea of the frame as a part of the piece, and the visual idea of some elements moving beyond the frame border."

Why, Why, Why, Delilah? (*See* Plate 38) represents the theme of betrayal and resultant catastrophe suggested by the biblical story the title alludes to. Here the frame, made of red-and-white-painted metal, is an integral part of the piece. The sense of the disintegration of a previously stable order is emphasized by the presence of this border, while fragments that mimic this border (made of red and white Vitrolite glass) are strewn on the "fractured" mottled glass within the border. "What I was dealing with thematically was a destruction of sorts, a falling down of this fresco or wall surface — represented by the mottled green glass. The areas of clear glass repeat this idea of breakup." It's a striking work, one remote from the kind of prettiness or decorativeness people tend to associate with stained glass. Its theme is disturbing, yet the piece is colorful and the composition is intriguing, even exciting.

The piece seems to point in at least one direction Robez wants to take in the future, a direction natural for an artist who is adept at the full range of cold- and hot-worked glass technique. "I'm interested in more of a multi-media approach," Robez reveals. "I want to do more experimenting, make more mistakes, see what's up ahead. There's the danger, for an artist, of becoming too satisfied with something. Then you're no longer an artist."

He went on to make an observation on his region's glass scene: "Here in eastern Canada we have the melting pot for Europe's architectural approach and California's personal statement in glass. I expect interesting things from this area in the future."

While Robez himself has done some interesting architectural work and intends to do more in the future, his name has been made with his autonomous panels. Because he has involved himself in an extensive exhibition schedule, his work has been seen enough to be bought on a regular basis; certainly many makers of independent panels are in far less favorable positions. Still, most glass galleries — to say nothing of other types of art galleries — refrain from carrying flat-glass work, because it is not easily displayed. What keeps Robez working in the frustrating field of stained glass — a traditionally architectural field — given the irrepressible personalism of his approach and his uncommon talent for creating art objects of an intimate scale?

His response is, first, to reaffirm the things that attracted him to glass originally: the color possibilities of the material and the processes involved in working with it. Then he adds, "It's a medium that has not been utilized much in a contemporary way. There's a lot of ground-breaking still to be done. That's not to say I won't work in other media, because above all my desire is to express myself visually. But I think I can say with confidence that I'll never forsake glass."

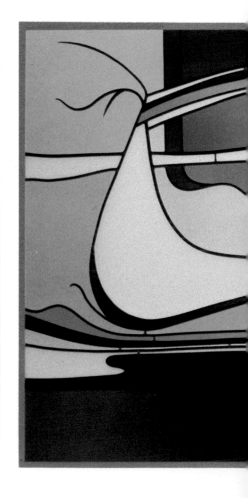

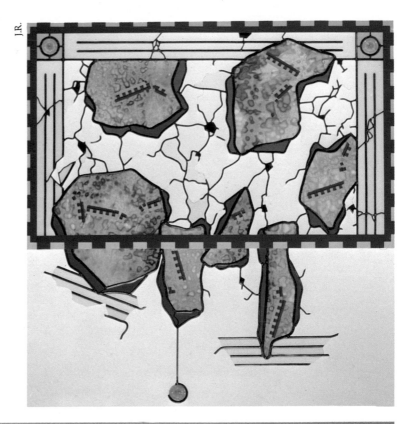

PLATE 37: (Below) *Outer Space*, 1982. 96 × 44 in. (243.8 × 111.8 cm) Collection of artist.

PLATE 38: (Right) *Why, Why, Why, Delilah?*, 1984. 42 × 43 in. (106.7 × 109.2 cm) Collection of artist.

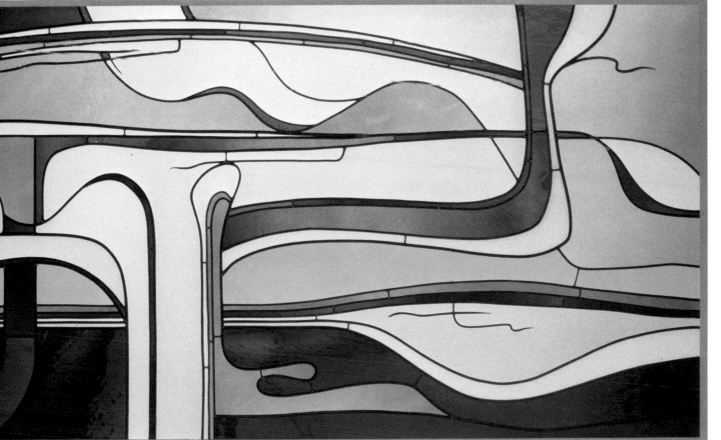

Rejene Stowe

The strong assemblage of rectilinear shapes at times seems flat and at other times appears to constitute a peculiar perspective on some architectonic structure. Its orderliness and its straight lines, combined with its blue and gray hues, give it a quiet autonomy. It lives in a world of mind.

It is *Reticulum* (*See* Plate 39): an independent stained-glass panel made in 1983 by Halifax-based artist Rejene Stowe.

"It was my reaction to moving to the city and feeling that wherever I looked there was some kind of very strong control of nature," she comments. "Even in a park, flowers and trees were planted in little neat rows. *Reticulum* is about the grid structures that our eyes are presented with all the time, which become so repetitive that they in turn influence what we are prepared to see. I tried to make the glass *not beautiful*, to look monotonous. But I found it was difficult to take all the visual appeal out of stained glass."

Stowe designed the panel shortly after moving to Halifax from Cape Breton Island. For some time she had lived in Red River, on Cape Breton Island, where she had settled after leaving the United States. She had made her home on a remote acreage in a rural neighborhood surrounded by wild nature. It was here, in 1973 — and out of sheer economic necessity — that she initially learned something about working in stained glass. Making "craft" items was at first purely a way to support herself, and for quite a while this was the limit of her interest. "I had seen virtually no stained glass in North America that excited me," she explains.

With her background, Stowe could readily have appreciated good work had she been exposed to it. Prior to her immigration to Canada in 1971, she had pursued a minor in art history during her years as a student at Lake Forest College in Illinois (where she majored in philosophy). While visiting

JOEL RUSS

Halifax in 1975, on a city sojourn from her Cape Breton home, she was approached by someone who had seen some of her commercial glass work and wanted her to participate in a show at Mount St. Vincent University Gallery. The woman also showed Stowe a magazine article on contemporary German architectural glass. "That was the first time I saw work by Schaffrath," she says. "I said to myself, 'There is something to stained glass, after all!' "

Stowe has regarded herself as a serious designer of stained glass since 1979. She studied with Johannes Schreiter — the glass designer whom she regards as the greatest single influence on her work — at the Pilchuck School of Glass in Washington State, in 1981, and again in Toronto, in 1984. She also studied briefly with Jochem Poensgen in Toronto in 1983. Stowe now feels that although the celebrated contemporary German glass designers opened her eyes, she has moved away from their influence to follow her own artistic vision.

In 1983 Stowe designed some interesting independent panels that openly acknowledged the German influence in expressing the artist's perception of the Halifax environment. These panels compose the triptych titled *The Light Screen Series* (See Plate 40). The titles of the individual panels in the series — "Homage to Schaffrath," "Homage to Poensgen," and "Homage to Schreiter" — suggest Stowe's sense of indebtedness to these contemporary masters of stained glass. Readers who are familiar with the work of these designers may find the subtle influence of each of these artists on the panel named for him. In "Homage to Schreiter," for example, the design is overlaid with erratic lines that Stowe derived from sketches she made of decaying leaves.

The Light Screen Series actually came out of the same period of adaptation to new surroundings that produced *Reticulum*.

PLATE 39: (Overleaf) *Reticulum*, 1983. 31 × 21 in. (78.7 × 53.3 cm) Collection of Nova Scotia Designer Craftsmen, Halifax, N.S. *Photograph by Andrew Terris.*

"The panels make reference to the dramatic changes in light that can occur from moment to moment in a coastal area — abrupt shifts from somberness, to clarity, to brilliance. Each panel contains something of each of these qualities, but the emphasis is different from one to another. I kept the lines as simple as possible, to draw attention to the light illuminating the design. The lines might also be seen as diagrams for city systems, in which the same basic pattern is presented repetitiously, with only slight modulations indicating uniqueness."

The limited color range in *Reticulum* and *The Light Screen Series* is fairly congruent with the rest of Stowe's work, because one of her dominant concerns has been to draw the viewer's attention to the interplay of light and glass. "When I use color in my work," she says, "it's in a very low-key way. I don't like to excite emotion. I like very, very quiet stained glass. But that doesn't mean I like *weak* work."

Stowe's major source of inspiration is nature, though this may not be readily evident. "One of the most breathtaking things where I live is to go out every day and watch the changes in the clouds and light. It's amazingly moving," she says. "I wanted to bring that into my work, but I wanted to avoid emotional appeal, because I didn't want to get corny about it." She has chosen the option of taking an abstract and formalistic approach in which the glass could be used to suggest aspects of natural light. Here, it is a matter of nature stimulating the mind of the artist, or perhaps nature being adapted to the purposes of the artist, rather than of nature being *represented* by the artist.

Currently, Stowe designs both independent panels and architectural glass. The latter, of course, requires her to moderate her strong personal vision to meet the requirements of the situation and the desires of an architect or other client. Yet even when she has been willing to do this, the going has not always been easy. Part of the problem has been the incongruity between her formalistic work and what is conventionally expected from a woman artist. "A lot of architects have trouble accepting my work," she says. "The problem is that many architects think that art should reflect the intuitive, graceful, gracious side of life." Clearly, Stowe's work is more penetrating than that.

Most of Rejene Stowe's work fits into the new, thoroughly non-traditional, experimental realm of stained-glass design —glass as fine art, rather than glass as architectural element. Her interest in historical approaches to glass design has always been limited. However, she told us that she does follow the contemporary North American and European scenes through journals, and she enjoys opportunities to interact with some of the artists involved. She mentioned Canadian expatriates Doreen Balabanoff and Stuart Reid, along with American Sanford Barnett, as artists whose work she has particularly admired. In agreement with some other glass artists who find the independent panel a satisfying and legitimate medium for self-expression, Stowe told us that she thought there was a lot of room for information exchange between painters and stained-glass artists.

In looking at Stowe's work, with its precise composition and restrained coloration, it is natural to wonder what the artist's over-all intention has been. She has apparently been pursuing something very refined —one is almost tempted to say "distilled." In attempting to identify an underlying theme in her work, she says, "For a number of years it was *clarity*," then adds: "I'm not a terribly expressive person, but I love expressionistic work. If I were working in painting, I might

146 REJENE STOWE

A.T.

PLATE 40: *The Light Screen Series*, triptych. (Left) "Homage to Schaffrath," (middle) "Homage to Poensgen," and (right) "Homage to Schreiter," 1983. Each panel 25 × 37 in. (63.5 × 94 cm) Collection of Nova Scotia Museum, Halifax, N.S.

paint expressionistically. But the medium of stained glass is so materials-heavy that, in fact, you have to be very careful when you handle it. So I tend to make very careful statements, even though I'm not trying to preach clarity any more." At the time of the interview, it seemed that Stowe had developed a focused, elegantly spare style of design that she could apply to whatever theme she felt like approaching.

Stowe originally learned her glass technique from her partner, Andrew Terris, with whom she ran the craft business in Cape Breton (and with whom she still shares a studio). Terris, a glass sculptor and an interesting artist in his own right, originally taught her what technique he knew. At the time of the interview, Stowe favored the copper-foil construction technique for all work except sizable architectural pieces. "You can get very intricate with it, without the clunkiness of lead. In architectural work I've *had* to use lead. In some situations I've come to appreciate the heaviness of it in contrast to the transparency of glass."

Andrew Terris is still more of a technical adventurer than Stowe, and while Stowe occasionally adopts techniques that Terris has explored, most of her panels have been examples of the effective use of basic stained-glass techniques. However, she told us that she felt she wanted to explore the techniques of sandblasting and glass painting further in the future.

Stowe does not seem to lack for creative ideas. In fact, ideas seem to compete with one another in her mind for the chance to emerge. "I have several different ideas, at any given time, that I've developed to a certain extent, on paper or mentally," she says. "I let the one that wants to be made next come to the fore. If I wait too long between the time I start on it and the time I actually get down to resolving all the aspects of it, I have to be able to drop it and start on another one that is stronger." Sometimes she develops a design in terms of line, in which case she draws. At other times, when coloration is her primary concern, she utilizes design techniques like collage or painting to develop the idea. Often, she finds, she gets blocked at about the time the design is three-quarters or seven-eighths formed, so that the last bit takes two weeks to do. She may agonize over the details of a design right up to the moment when she solders the last joint in a panel.

Stowe has been nearly as interested in studying the creative process as she has been in designing panels. "I'm very interested in the process of making a work of art, what's actually happening to you psychologically when you sit down to design," she explains. "That in itself is so interesting that if I have any spare time, that's where I put my energy." Her study has not been merely academic in nature, for she has felt that if she could learn what blocks the creative process, she would know how to liberate it. More than anything else, her inquiry has been a study of the self.

"When I was designing *Reticulum*, I was working with the notion of trying to let go of too much conscious control in the work," she recalls. "Here the design had a message to give me, rather than my trying to communicate a message. I was accustomed to being in control and deciding in advance what was going to be said and carefully building up the elements from that base. Then came a critical moment when I realized that the design had a life of its own, and a struggle ensued because I was unwilling to give up conscious control. *Reticulum* was a model for a highly structured system that was both dynamic and dead — my *real* reaction to the city environment, rather than a consciously prettified 'statement.' "

In 1984 Stowe designed an independent panel of a very different character, a piece titled *Mysterium Coniunctionis* (See Plate 41). Robert Dietz, owner of Dresden Galleries, and the art dealer who represents Stowe's work, decided to mount an art exhibition to celebrate the Pope's visit to Halifax. The show, rather than being linked strictly to a particular religion or religious leader, was to be devoted to the theme of spirituality in a more open-ended way. Dietz felt that there were similarities between the esthetic and religious experiences, but that this was not widely appreciated in our society. He asked the artists who were to participate in the exhibition to attempt to bridge the gap between the two types of experience by making works that would represent a drawing together of the two, or would express spiritual feeling esthetically.

"I chose to work with the idea of the crucifixion, and the basic symbolism of the cross—a coming together of the mundane with the supramundane," Stowe explains. "To arrive at the verticals and horizontals, I contemplated for hours a

piece of masonite that was blank except for two shadow lines which barely suggested two limbs of a cross. I did numerous sketches of what I saw on the masonite. I photocopied these images and worked color into the piece in a rather traditional symbolic way.

"My approach to designing *Mysterium* was a bit more straightforward because I had learned so much about my own artistic process from *Reticulum*. I had learned to give up a lot of conscious control, but I still had a fascination with the process, and this fascination tended to slow me down considerably."

As she intimates here, Stowe worked out the coloring quite deliberately, and along traditional lines. The white area in the upper portion of the panel symbolizes transcendence. The purple in the lower area symbolizes sensuousness. The somber purple-gray and very deep wine-purple colors were used simply to provide background coloration. The vertical red stripes at the right refer to suffering. "The red that cuts across the middle of the panel is a strong and somewhat organic interruption of the more heavily structured forms," Stowe explains. "Where the structures attempt to come together in a new, solid formation, there's an interruption, a flash, a spark."

We might only add that this piece — with its rich, albeit judicious, coloration — burns with a quiet fire. It is very different in effect from Stowe's more nearly monochromatic works.

The fact is that Stowe's work is continually changing: evolving. "I feel that some well-known glass artists have backed themselves into a corner," she says. "I hope that I never get to the stage where I'm so known for a style that that's all I can do. On the other hand, some artists tend to go wide rather than deep.

"I know my work will be abstract for the rest of my life," Stowe quietly adds. "But I can see myself wanting to convey more organic images. Also, I want to see more spontaneity in terms of line in my work. I want to draw more and have the drawing there in my work, not left behind at the design stage."

Stowe's serious work to date has been uniquely affecting, and her future work promises to continue to combine subtlety of presentation with depth of vision.

PLATE 41: *Mysterium Coniunctionis*, 1984. 28 × 41 in. (71.1 × 104.1 cm) Collection of artist.

A.T.

Terry Smith-Lamothe

Color helps combat the gray bleakness of springtime here in Halifax. It's a medicinal potion for the March storms." Terry Smith-Lamothe is certainly not averse to using strong hues in his windows. He feels that his work communicates various things at different levels — and one of those things is pure joy, the kind of blithe feeling one has on a warm, sunny day.

Perhaps Smith-Lamothe's colorful windows are his way of importing a bit of subtropical *soleil* to his Maritime home. In moving to Nova Scotia from the United States, the artist has retraced the steps of his Acadian ancestors, who settled in Louisiana where Smith-Lamothe was born and raised.

Smith-Lamothe's routes to both Nova Scotia and stained glass were circuitous ones. While majoring in psychology at Louisiana State University in 1972, he took a course in pottery and showed some raku work in a student art exhibit. Yet despite the interest he had had since childhood in things creative, he could not at this time imagine an art career for himself. Still, the breathtaking impact of the stained glass he saw (in cathedrals in, for example, Stuttgart and Milan) while traveling in Europe in 1969 had not faded from his memory. Among the examples of stained glass that he enjoyed most were works of modern German masters in cathedrals rebuilt after World War II.

After graduating from Louisiana State, Smith-Lamothe pursued graduate studies in a Unitarian theological seminary — the Thomas S. King School for Religious Leadership — in Berkeley, California. During this period he supported himself as a telephone crisis-line counselor and as a paramedic. Leaving Berkeley, still in search of new experiences, Smith-Lamothe immigrated to Canada in 1973 to live the homesteading life near Oxford, Nova Scotia.

JOEL RUSS

While sojourning in Mississippi in 1979, Smith-Lamothe's wife, Judith, took an introductory stained-glass course and passed along the technical rudiments to Terry. He looks back on this as the point at which the artistic-leaning side of his nature began to overpower the "practical" side. Soon, though, he began to suspect there might be some practical possibilities hidden within this new interest. "I saw in it a means for self-expression, and also maybe a way to support myself," he relates. "I gave away my first piece, but sold my second." Smith-Lamothe discovered that he had some natural ability with the graphic aspect of stained-glass design. It soon became clear to him where he wanted to take this art form. "I was old enough at the time to know that I didn't want to do production stained glass. What I wanted to do were serious, large windows."

His study of stained glass and its functions became intensive. He took a quick architecture course at a technical college and began to pore over books and journals devoted to the medium. At various times he studied briefly with Robert Jekyll, Kenneth vonRoenn, Ray King, and Jochem Poensgen. Gradually he began to get the sort of architectural commissions that he had set his sights on.

St. Stephen's Catholic Church in Halifax (*See* Plate 42) offers an example of the irrepressible buoyancy of Smith-Lamothe's approach to architectural glass. The artist was commissioned in 1982 to design windows to replace the old, deteriorating fenestration in this church situated in a Catholic neighborhood. Smith-Lamothe presented to the church committee drawings based on two design directions: one was a traditional and more symmetrical approach; the other was freer, more contemporary, but still figurative. The committee preferred the latter, as did the artist. Smith-Lamothe

PLATE 42: (Left) St. Stephen's Catholic Church, 1982. "Pentecost" window, 43 × 104 in. (109.2 × 264.2 cm) Halifax, N.S.

PLATE 43: (Below) *Continental Drift*, 1981. 21 × 51 in. (53.3 × 129.5 cm) Collection of Nova Scotia Department of Culture, Recreation and Fitness.

derived his themes for the ten windows in the church's east and west walls from New Testament scenes, and in the installed windows these scenes appear in a sequence that follows the chronological order in which they are given in the Gospels. The artist incorporated traditional Catholic symbolism in the windows: blue clothing for the Virgin; certain hand gestures for the figure of Jesus; a purple robe for the angel Gabriel, and so on. But another symbolic level is inherent in the fact that the artist deliberately used transparent glass, so that parishioners could look through the windows to their neighborhood outside.

One's first impression upon entering the church in the afternoon is of the dazzling color of the windows and the joyful atmosphere the light coming through them creates in the church as a whole. The strength of the simple forms, with the organic quality of their outlines, is apparent upon closer study of individual windows. It seems that Smith-Lamothe has very effectively brought the church into the late twentieth century.

With reference to the symbolic content of such works as his St. Stephen's Church windows, Smith-Lamothe comments: "Stained glass, since the Middle Ages, has served a didactic purpose through the use of symbols. Stained glass in secular buildings has served to evoke sentiments, and symbols have always been an aspect of this function." While many contemporary glass artists resist the idea of working symbols into their designs, preferring to work totally abstractly, Smith-Lamothe finds the subject of symbolism intriguing at least in part because of his study (as a psychology major at university) of Carl Jung's theories about symbols and their relation to the collective unconscious.

Though church windows constitute only a portion of Smith-Lamothe's output, most of his work has been architectural glass of some sort. He estimates that roughly one-third of his

TERRY SMITH-LAMOTHE 155

work is done in cooperation with architects. "I've usually had restrictions on my style," he admits. "It's been rare for someone to say to me, 'I want you to make a window for me. I don't care what you do.'" When it has appeared that the compromises in a job at hand would be too great, he has felt compelled to refuse the commission.

Smith-Lamothe's window *Continental Drift* (*See* Plate 43) was not as yet installed when we interviewed him. It was designed for a building belonging to the Nova Scotia Department of Culture, Recreation and Fitness. Smith-Lamothe designed the window to fit a frame he had on hand (one that, interestingly, came from a convent in Saskatchewan that was demolished in 1906). As to the theme he chose for the window, the artist comments: "The design represents the drifting apart of the continents, with the presence of a mid-ocean ridge of higher geologic activity." On the level of direct visual effect, Smith-Lamothe wanted to impress the viewer with the languid flowing together of the lead and glass. Since the window would be set in a west wall, he intended an image of colored light to cross the floor and be reflected part way up the east wall, spreading the continental drift theme across the room. However this might work out, the deep-blue German antique glass (used to represent the ocean) and the streaky warm-toned glass (representing the land masses) give the window itself a rich depth.

Though he has had experience with a wide range of techniques in glass surface treatment and panel construction, to date Smith-Lamothe has mostly relied on conventional techniques in executing his works. He estimates that 95 percent of his construction has been carried out using lead cames. "I like the way you can change the width of the line, which is not easy to do with copper foil. Also, I think that leading is faster than copper-foil construction. And with lead I feel a sense of spiritual connection with the medieval artist who used the same materials."

Given the complexity and fussiness of the stained-glass fabrication process, it can be difficult to strictly translate a design idea, in its pure form, into an actual panel. The artist's comments on how he deals with the technical limitations of the medium are revealing: "Well, you design the window first. Then you figure out how to make it. I enjoy the challenge. If I wanted to do an oil painting, I'd do an oil painting, not try to do one with stained glass." In other words, if one loves the medium, one accepts and works with, not against, its limitations.

Smith-Lamothe has taught continually since he established himself as a stained-glass artist in Halifax. Besides passing on his knowledge of stained-glass technique, he has explored the history of the medium with his students, a process that he has found very valuable personally. At the time that we interviewed him, Smith-Lamothe was serving as the current president of the Atlantic Glass Artisans, a Halifax-based association that organizes workshops, exhibitions, and other events for serious amateur and professional artists. He has done some of his teaching through AGA, but teaches on a more regular basis through the extension program of the Nova Scotia College of Art and Design.

At this point, Smith-Lamothe has come a long way from both Louisiana and crisis-line counseling. Yet perhaps it is not too far-fetched to speculate that he has consciously attempted to bring a dimension of soul healing to the good people of Halifax through his ebullient stained-glass windows.

Warren Carther

M y work is experimental," declares Warren Carther. "Up to now stained glass has been kept in the shackles of tradition. I try to push glass to its limits. I don't think I've ever made a piece without trying something new technically."

When Carther resettled himself in Winnipeg a few years ago, with a solid ten years of training in art and glass-working, he was certainly well equipped to embark on a creative exploration of the glass medium. Carther started studying art in high school. He first became interested in glass in 1972, while a student of sculpture at the University of Manitoba. Initially, as a result of seeing an impressive blown-glass lamp in the Winnipeg Art Gallery, he was excited by the idea of doing hot-glass sculptural work. Instructors at the university suggested that he study at Naples Mill School of Arts and Crafts, in New York State, where glass-blowing was taught in the curriculum. He spent some profitable weeks in that school's summer program in 1974, then returned to the University of Manitoba for the following school year. When he learned of the reputation of the California College of Arts and Crafts, he applied for admission to its glass program, was accepted, and moved down to northern California's East Bay area.

"When I got there, I found it was absolutely fantastic!" Carther remembers. "It was a school that taught everything imaginable about glass, though it was primarily set up to deal with blown glass—which was what I was interested in at the time. But there were a few people working in stained glass in the school then. Richard Posner was a graduate student there at the time. The first time I was around anyone making a stained-glass window was when Richard was making a window called *Another Look at My Beef with the Government*. I held some glass while he was breaking some large pieces. Up until then I hadn't known what could be done with flat glass."

PLATE 44: Stairwell window, Lynch residence, 1982. 30 × 64 in. (76.2 cm × 162.6 cm) Vancouver, B.C.

J.R.

Carther became fascinated with the possibilities of stained glass because it offered the artist more complete control than did the hot-glass medium.

Carther studied at the college in 1976–77. And, since he was living in northern California, he was in the fortunate position of being able to meet the luminaries of the West Coast "New Glass" movement, among them Paul Marioni, Peter Mollica, Dan Fenton, Kathie Stackpole Bunnell, and Sanford Barnett. "There were so many stained-glass artists there, I would have been extremely foolish to have left that area and not taken the opportunity of meeting them."

Carther graduated from the California College of Arts and Crafts with a bachelor's degree in fine arts. Just after graduation, he received a letter from the University of Manitoba offering him a position as the stained-glass instructor in the summer program. When he left California for Winnipeg, he had already installed his first architectural glass commission, work that he described as having a "marginal German influence" in it.

Back in Winnipeg, Carther set up a well-equipped stained-glass studio at the university. He taught through the university during four summer sessions and, after that, taught a studio program through the Winnipeg Art Gallery for several years. During the same period, he was taking architectural commissions, and, he says, often found teaching a distraction from his own work. "I felt lucky to have one good student a year," he recalls.

Carther's work has been mostly architectural, much of it stained glass for residential situations. A duplex in Point Grey, Vancouver, contains some excellent examples. The stairwell window (See Plate 44) in the Lynch residence appears entirely non-objective at first, but actually represents one of Carther's favorite themes: window. The composition is basically simple, with large expanses of sandblasted antique glass and a pattern of slatlike bands of brown glass in the middle area suggesting venetian blinds. Looking at the piece for a few moments, the perceptive viewer will notice an abstract shape, in the lower right-hand area of the panel, suggestive of a human head. Is it, or isn't it? Carther confirms the suspicion, saying that he likes to refer to such recurring figures in his work as "ambiguites [sic]." The situation cryptically depicted is one of a person peeking through venetian blinds.

On the technical level, this window is interesting for Carther's deft and diverse uses of sandblasting. Not only has he used the technique here to frost much of the glass, thus softening its appearance and insuring privacy for the home's occupants, he has also used it to penetrate the glass, to put a precisely shaped hole in the large sheet of white glass at the top of the window; this allowed him to splice in other glass, so that the venetian-blind pattern appears to peep through.

Among the things that lie behind Carther's fascination with the window as a *subject* is his experience of northern California lifestyles. He noticed that in Berkeley, where many of the homes are situated near the sidewalks, people's lifestyles were on display in what amounted to a fascinating form of social communication. House windows would exhibit such things as plants, or flags, or *objets d'art*, or crafted items, in a fashion that was a statement, at once casual and deliberate, about the occupants' identity. In part, this phenomenon prompted Carther's interest in the window as a metaphor for looking into different worlds. Carther's sandblasted windows often include one or more areas of transparent glass that represent a conventional, transparent window, and thus embody this metaphor. He often refers to these areas as "graphic illustrations of windows."

Yet Carther doesn't generally like to explain his design ideas. He feels that ambiguous elements help the viewer to feel an excitement of discovery in viewing his windows that is similar to the excitement he experiences in designing them. Among the few other clues he will offer on the subject of his designs is the fact that musical elements — rhythm and harmony — are important influences in his work (he often designs with music playing in his studio).

An example of Carther's larger-scale work is also to be found in the three-story Point Grey duplex. Carther designed an expanse of windows that stretches across the building's rear wall, then wraps around the corner for several feet at each end. The combined length of these panels is twenty-five feet, eight inches. The windows form what are essentially stained-glass walls in the bathrooms on the second floor of the duplex's two dwellings. "Since the windows ran from one house into the other," Carther points out, "I had the unique challenge of designing windows that would work when looked at from the inside, where [only] half the window would be seen, and from the outside, where you'd see all of the window. The glass was sandblasted for privacy, except for some very small, sort of rectangular areas of transparent glass. You could put your face up to these little areas and look out into the yard, yet the window provides a perfect screen from the outside." Again the window-within-window motif.

The glass in these second-floor bathrooms does work to excellent effect both esthetically and in the preservation of privacy. The bathroom in the Cox residence (*See* Plate 45) is a veritable stained-glass environment. With their irregular

PLATE 45: (Overleaf) Bathroom window, Cox residence, 1982. Section of window, 25.5 × 4.5 ft. (7.77 × 1.37 m) Vancouver, B.C. *Photograph by Joel Russ.*

lines and large pieces of glass, these windows are somewhat suggestive of landforms. Irregularity, or "organic line," is dominant in the over-all design, with straight lines and other geometric elements playing more limited, though essential roles. One interesting aspect of these windows is the leadline overlays, both straight and irregular, that jut or meander into the large, softly colored glass shapes, playing no structural role. Other points of interest are the three circles of fused glass in the panel on the right; the three small collapsed squares in the panel on the left (the transparent areas to which Carther referred); and the deep-carved sandblasted areas in the brown glass in the lower left-hand corner of the panel on the left.

Just as in the Cox residence, the glass in the Lynch bathroom creates a stained-glass environment. The Lynch residence also contains examples of Carther's work in other contexts that are no less interesting. The stairwell window we discussed earlier is one example. Another, the small window in the second-floor den (*See* Plate 46), adds a subtle accent to a pleasant living space. Except for an area in the upper right-hand corner, the window's originally transparent glass has been heavily frosted by sandblasting. Again Carther made a number of perforations in the window by sandblasting all the way through the glass; he then filled these holes with colored, transparent antique glass, once again playing on the window-within-window idea. The window is engaging to look at, while its simplicity of design makes it easy to live with.

Carther seems very western in his approach to stained-glass design. This is, of course, partly explained by the formative period the artist spent in northern California. His work represents an evocative visual poetry of a particular flavor, and this is more a matter of an artistic sensibility than a matter of particular design or assembly techniques; hence, it is difficult to define. Still, certain specific characteristics can be identified. There is the undertone of things natural suggested by the dominance of hand-drawn, organic line. There is also the sense of spaciousness—conveyed by the use of large pieces of glass — that is characteristic of the Manitoba landscape, as well as of the outdoorsy lifestyle that pervades the west. Also, Carther usually works with a limited palette, with simple and pleasing color harmonies, and often with gentle hues that result from sandblasting antique glass; there is no trace of bustle, discord, or overload in his windows. Though Carther's glass works well in the buildings of the western cities in which it is installed, his work is not "urbane" in quite the way that much of the work being done in the East is. We find this an interesting contrast.

Carther's technical explorations have always been intertwined with the development of his design ideas, and technical discovery has always excited him. Soon after his initiation into stained glass, he explored photo-etching, a technique whereby a photograph can be transferred into the glass surface. Early on he worked with acid etching as a way to incise patterns deeply into glass, though later he substituted deep sandblasting for this technique, for health reasons. He makes extensive use of sandblasting, a technique that he controls masterfully. Carther also makes much use of glass fusing, in order to eliminate the leadline between areas of colored glass or, more often, to build up layers of glass for surface-relief effects. Indeed, because of his increasing use of various relief techniques, he feels his glass work is in a curious way moving back toward the hot-glass sculptural work he began with.

PLATE 46: (Left) Den of Lynch residence, 1982. 33 × 41 in. (83.8 × 104.1 cm) Vancouver, B.C.

PLATE 47: (Below) Study window, Teichman residence, 1981. 51 × 44 in. (129.5 × 111.8 cm) Winnipeg, Manitoba.

D.T.   J.R.

The study window in the Teichman residence (*See* Plate 47) incorporates several of Carther's favorite techniques. The background is sandblasted clear glass, frosted so that it appears luminous white in daylight. In the upper right are inset one complete rectangle and one partial rectangle of magenta antique glass, through which the trees and other aspects of the yard outside can be seen. On the panel's left is a meandering, partially divided, striped patch. Each of the horizontal bars of transparent blue glass that Carther used in this section he made by fusing four layers of glass strips in a kiln; the resulting thick, round-edged, half-inch-wide bars were then assembled using half-inch-wide lead cames, resulting in a banded effect. The "bas-relief" technique gives the section a pronounced ribbed quality. Aside from these points of special technical interest, the window is a good example of quiet composition that is pleasant to live with at close quarters.

At this point, Warren Carther has a strong identity in stained glass. When we interviewed him, his enthusiasm for the potential of glass as a creative medium did not seem to have cooled since the days of his early ardor. "I think glass is one of the most beautiful materials the world has ever seen," he declares. "Glass can do things that no other material can do. It can be flowing and liquid or rigid and hard, soft or brittle, sharp or smooth, translucent or opaque. It can be brightly colored, or it can be pretty without any color at all. How can I help but want to use it to make art?"

Brian Baxter

Brian Baxter usually walks from his apartment to his studio in the morning, partly for the exercise and partly to savor the ambience of Vancouver. He left Halifax, where he attended art school, specifically because he wanted to live in a larger urban community. "I still enjoy living in the city, because of the movement and vitality, the concentration of people, and the fact that people are always changing images," he says.

JOEL RUSS

At his studio he often designs or constructs his artworks in glass to a background of radio music — frequently rhythm and blues, or popular music that leans toward the *avant-garde*. He starts work early, usually finishing by late afternoon. He feels he is at his most creative early in the day.

Although it seems inevitable that Baxter became an artist, it appears strictly fortuitous that he became a glass artist. A native of Nova Scotia, he recognized his artistic inclination while an adolescent. He studied commercial art at the Nova Scotia College of Art and Design and, during his last year at the college, went to Europe on a "World Encounter" travel/study program. What he was able to learn firsthand about European history and culture made sense of the European art he had previously only studied academically. Baxter graduated from the college in 1973 with a degree in graphic design.

Later, after he had moved to Vancouver, Baxter found himself in need of a job. The Canada Manpower office directed him to a studio that was interested in training someone in the skills of stained-glass window repair. But when he followed up the referral, he found that the job opening no longer existed. By now, however, he was finding the notion of working with stained glass intriguing. He checked with several other stained-glass studios and found one that could use a helper. So in May 1977, Baxter commenced his apprentice-ship in stained glass at a studio in Vancouver. The next year, he continued his apprenticeship at another commercially oriented stained-glass studio in Port Moody, B.C.

Given his artistic inclination and training, it was inevita-ble that Baxter would invest this medium with more-than-commercial significance. In his search for an esthetic through which to make personally meaningful visual statements, Baxter evolved through a series of influences: Art Nouveau, particularly what he terms the ''more masculine'' styles of Charles Rennie Mackintosh and Josef Hoffmann; Art Deco in general; Japanese art in general. But during these formative phases, Baxter's designs were both fairly derivative and largely representational.

Not until a three-week studio session, in 1980, with the prominent California stained-glass artist Narcissus Quagliata, at the Pilchuck School of Glass in Washington State, did Baxter begin to feel truly emancipated in his artistic evolu-tion. He views Quagliata as a natural teacher or guide who respects the personal inclinations of those he teaches. "When I came back from that studio session, I felt liberated," Baxter says. "It was through Narcissus that I got into doing abstract work in a serious way." When one considers that nearly all the well-known work of Quagliata himself is representational rather than abstract, Baxter's statement seems a consider-able tribute to his instructor.

Baxter's current work is thoroughly urbane and progres-sive, informed both by what is new and exciting in the field of graphic design, and by a vital originality of its own. Al-though Baxter is most free in his independent work, he adapts his ideas to the requirements of architectural situations when he takes on a commission. On the architectural side, Baxter's portfolio includes work in both residences and public buildings.

Baxter's work has developed rapidly in the last few years — so much so that he has lost interest in much of his early architectural work. But among the residential windows that he is still fond of are those in a Vancouver residence. The window in the bathroom of the house (*See* Plate 48) is an intimate piece measuring twenty by thirty-one inches. The design gives the impression of a set of venetian blinds at the moment of being ripped asunder or burst through — a wry jest, in a bathroom window. (The client had wanted a window that would provide both the necessary privacy and a limited view of the garden. Knowing her to have a good sense of humor, Baxter came up with this design.) Again following the client's wishes, Baxter incorporated some of the colors from the room's wallpaper in the window. He achieved the "blinds" effect mostly through the use of sandblasted clear glass, which appears white. He used colored glass for the shading of the ruptured ends. The reamy antique clear glass in the center provides an interesting contrast to the sandblasted glass.

The main directions of Baxter's current work branch away from what is ordinarily recognized as stained glass. In fact, the artist says that he is interested in getting rid of the "stained-glass" label. The untitled independent panel (*See* Plate 49) is colorless in itself, picking up color only from what lies behind and in front of the piece. This is because, in the artist's view, "the beauty of glass is in texture and light, not color." The technique here is still the traditional leaded-glass approach, with lead cames of different widths used for interest and balance. Several types of textured commercial glass were used — though sparingly — in the piece; sandblasting was used more extensively, various pieces of glass being frosted to different degrees. In this piece, the artist says, he was trying to

PLATE 48: Bathroom window in private residence, 1981. 20 × 31 in. (50.8 × 78.7 cm) Vancouver, B.C.

J.R.

achieve an effect of various planes of depth. The angularity of this composition of lines and apparent planes is quite provocative.

At the time of the interview, Baxter had an untitled panel on display at a Vancouver gallery. The piece was actually designed to be built as a bathroom window, but had not yet been installed. This virtually colorless panel (*See* Plate 50) is again designed with straightforward geometries, the composition being essentially based on concentric squares. The other elements that come into play — the rectangle, the triangle, and the straight line — are all used overtly and give the impression of being casually, even randomly arranged. At first glance, the border around the inmost square seems to have a haphazardly cross-hatched pattern; but on closer study this proves to be composed of various out-of-phase "layers" of quite regular, perpendicular cross-hatching. The over-all effect of this collage in glass is bold and upbeat.

There is an interesting technical side to this thoroughly non-traditional panel. The foundation glass, in which most of the visible pattern has been produced, started out as a square sheet of mirror glass. Baxter sandblasted away the silver backing, except in those areas to which he applied various resists (areas which tend to appear black in the photograph). The cross-hatch pattern surrounding the center square, for example, was made by using industrial wire screen as a resist. The group of appliquéd glass triangles on the bottom left are given extra depth by the fact that they appear to be casting shadows; the "shadows" are actually intact areas of silvering, left by a carefully placed resist during the sandblasting process. The only color in the panel comes from whatever is reflected by the intact areas of silvering or subtly filtered through the sandblasted glass.

Many of Baxter's latest pieces are not intended to transmit light at all, only to reflect it. Consequently, they are patently outside the sphere of stained glass. "The reflected-light pieces that I do are intended to force people to look at the medium of glass in its purest terms," Baxter points out. "You're not looking through them. You have to concentrate on the glass." These pieces, therefore, constitute a kind of commentary on the material itself. Clearly, Brian Baxter is an artist who works *at times* in stained glass; he can no longer be labeled "a stained-glass artist." His work promises to inhabit those areas where traditional glass arts meet very contemporary mixed-media formats.

PLATE 49: (Left) Untitled, 1981. 22 × 41 in. (55.9 × 104.1 cm) Private collection.

PLATE 50: (Right) Untitled, 1984. 24 × 24 in. (61 × 61 cm) Private residence.

174 BRIAN BAXTER

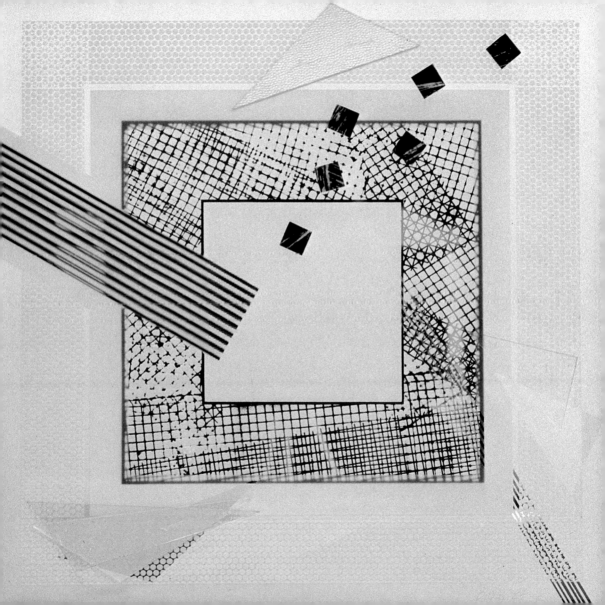

Stephen Taylor

There was a twentieth-century English artist, I can't remember who, who said you do best getting your training in a bad art school — mainly because you come out without any influences. For instance, if you went to Hornsey in North London, they could recognize you as a Hornsey student for three hundred miles. Wimbledon Art School was a lousy art school. It taught you the basics. The only sane place in there was the stained-glass department.''

It happens to have been the department in which British-born artist Stephen Taylor got his start in stained glass. His expressed opinion of the school may be somewhat tongue-in-cheek, since from his description of his experiences at Wimbledon from 1955 to 1960 he appears to have acquired a fairly solid grounding in art. In his first two years he took instruction not only in such "backbone" courses as drawing, painting, and art history, but also in the disciplines of printmaking, graphic design, and stained glass. The stained-glass instructor was young and open-minded and the department's students were among the school's *avant-garde*. After his second year, Taylor specialized in painting for a while and then switched his specialty to stained glass, still continuing studies in painting and printmaking.

"About my second year at Wimbledon, a good friend of mine was really into Oskar Kokoschka," Taylor told us. "Kokoschka's landscape paintings seemed to me to be the ultimate. Still do. I'd steal one tomorrow, if I had half a chance. Kokoschka was the man who had the major influence on my paintings. But as Lawrence Lee used to say, you assimilate your master's best and bury it in your own work."

Lawrence Lee, among the most celebrated contemporary British stained-glass designers, was one of the three artists who designed the ten 70-foot-high nave windows in Coventry Cathedral. Lee was Taylor's instructor at the renowned Royal College of Art in Kensington Gore, to which Taylor was admitted in 1961. He entered the college after he had spent six months traveling in France to study architecture and architectural stained glass.

"I got into the college on strange terms," he recalls. "We had to submit work, and we had to go through a bloody hard three-day entrance exam. There were a hundred and four applicants for four places in the stained-glass department, and I didn't have the equivalent of Canadian Grade Thirteen. Years later, when Lawrence Lee became a good friend, I asked him: 'Why did you accept me? I didn't come up to the criteria.' He said, 'No, you didn't. But you had *something*: potential. I had been teaching long enough to know you'd be one of the few here to continue doing stained glass.' He figured about one in thirty-five students would continue."

Taylor's studies under Lee were an extension of what he had learned at Wimbledon, although there was a stronger emphasis on architectural stained glass at the Royal College of Art — and also on free experimentation. He finished at the college in 1964, but after a year spent driving a truck, he was back at stained glass, working as Lawrence Lee's studio director. Taylor was in charge of the fabrication of four large stained-glass windows for St. Luke's Church in Norwood, Surrey. He also helped with the installation of these windows, which was being handled by the expert Limes Glass Works, of Oxted, Surrey. Because Taylor's skills in installation were at this point limited, Lee had obtained a position for him with Limes, where Taylor worked for six months. As a result of his training there, Taylor soon became known as a competent supervisor of glass installations. Also through Lee, Taylor met glass designer John Hayward, at whose studio he

PLATE 51: (Overleaf) Detail of Baptistry window showing Taylor's glass-painting technique, Holy Angels Church, 1974. Etobicoke, Ontario. *Photograph by Joel Russ.*

began to work in 1966. At Hayward's studio he worked on some immense commissions for Blackburn Cathedral.

Taylor speaks very warmly of both Lee and Hayward. "They were like fathers to their students, and they would come down with a very heavy stick if they felt you were throwing your talent away. You were there for art, and that was it. It was a kind of intensity that seems to have vanished."

When Taylor came to Canada, in 1968, in search of career opportunity, he brought with him what would have been, in other societal contexts, impressive qualifications in an important field of art. The problem was that the North American stained-glass revival had not yet begun, and there were few professional studios to work in. However, before he left England, Taylor had made arrangements by correspondence to work in the studio of the pioneer of modern Canadian stained glass, Yvonne Williams. Taylor again alludes to what he regards as a departed intensity among artists when he recalls his first days working in the Toronto studio of the now-elderly glass designer. "When I came here and started sweeping Yvonne Williams's studio, I didn't care that I was only making $2.50 an hour. It was being in a studio." Taylor eventually became Williams's studio manager.

Taylor worked part-time in Williams's studio from 1968 until the end of 1981. After a frustrating first year in Canada, he began to develop relationships of his own with some architects and started getting his own commissions. In the fifteen years since that point, most of his work has been for churches, and this, of course, has been very much in line with the training and experience he got in England.

Of all the artists represented in this book, Stephen Taylor takes the most painterly technical approach by far. In his work he has nearly always prepared the colored glass pieces of his windows by painting virtually every one of them with enamels, a technique still much used in Britain and France. More basic, perhaps, his compositional approach is a painterly one. Taylor is, after all, a trained easel painter as well as a stained-glass artist, and during his years at Wimbledon Art School his favorite artists were painters.

Looking at Taylor's windows, with their characteristic, well-controlled composition and their strong and varied color laid down in bits reminiscent of a painter's brush strokes, it is perhaps tempting to propose a connection with the Oskar Kokoschka landscapes that the artist so much admires. Along with the German Expressionist movement in general, Taylor also mentions Léger, Matisse, Manessier, the young Picasso, and Soutine as individual painters he has been particularly interested in. Influences from artists like these have probably contributed to the development of Taylor's style. Yet to a North American eye, Taylor's often lyrical and usually deeply colored approach has a stronger affinity to the tradition of the British and French stained-glass designers who have also used the glass-painting technique both for shading effects and to control the light transmitted by specific areas of a window.

A detail of the baptistry window in Holy Angels Church in Etobicoke, Ontario (*See* Plate 51), illustrates how Taylor uses the glass-painting technique. In this example, the paint serves several functions. One is to accentuate the lines of the window's leading. Related to this is the effect of enhanced visual depth that the enamel brushwork provides. Yet another function is the subduing of light that would otherwise stream intensely through the glass. Taylor has, of course, spent a long time perfecting his use of glass painting. "When I look back on what I did in England, the painting was incredibly crude," he muses with a smile. "It had a raw vitality to it, but it was not quite so strong as the present work."

We asked Taylor why he continues to exploit the painting technique when so few Canadian glass artists use it to any considerable extent. "I haven't seen the technique exhausted," he replies, "though many people put down the idea of painting glass. I frankly find it a hell of a challenge. But Lawrence Lee had an important rule that I still observe: every piece of glass in the window has to have an area of pure color coming through, even if it's just a pinprick."

In 1970 Taylor was commissioned for the first of three thematic windows he was to design for Holy Angels Church in Etobicoke, Ontario. Three years later he designed the third, the north window (*See* Plate 52), and was given the rather difficult and somewhat unusual theme of immigration to work with. "I saw the idea of riverlike forms meeting, flowing in from different directions. The central part of this window is a large protective form, into which these shapes converge," he explains. Then he adds, "The window is probably the most non-representational I've ever done."

Taylor took a brightly colored approach, but used a restricted palette. The window is regarded by some other artists who have seen it as Taylor's most Canadian work, though he had been in Canada for only a few years when he designed it. He recalls that stained-glass artist Sarah Hall told him that the design reminded her of a totem pole.

"The opportunity in stained glass for me is still in the Church," Taylor remarks. Though he has done some secular jobs, church glass is the sort of work he was trained in before he came to Canada, and he seems to be most comfortable with it. Taylor has established a reputation for excellent original work in the field of ecclesiastical glass in eastern Canada.

PLATE 52: *Immigration window*, Holy Angels Church, 1974. 3 × 8 ft. (.91 × 2.44 m) Etobicoke, Ontario.

J.R.

The chancel window (six feet, ten inches in diameter) in St. Mark's United Church in Scarborough, Ontario (*See* Plate 53), present another strong design. "This wall faces southeast, and every Sunday morning the minister was being barbecued," Taylor recalls. "So the church committee wanted a window that would be a light stopper." The artist chose a deeply saturated purple for the background, so as to add detail to the design and to reduce the amount of light coming through the glass. As a point of interest, the modeling of the crown of thorns should be noted.

In addition to limiting the light coming through the southeast window, the panel was, in its design, supposed to symbolize rebirth — spiritual renewal and the renewal of the Church. "The fire symbol at the bottom, rising up into a chalice and going out into a sort of aura, symbolizes the idea of rebirth," Taylor explains.

As the practical requisites of the St. Mark's window point out, Taylor's considerations in designing stained glass go beyond design esthetics and thematic function. Just how the building is used and where the people in it will be located in relation to the stained glass is of essential concern to Taylor. "Stained glass, for me, has always been a matter of relating directly to architecture. To me, that's the essence." Balancing theme and esthetics with architectural realities is not an easy task, and Taylor has sometimes turned down jobs when he didn't respect the architecture of a building.

Taylor was commissioned to do the east window (*See* Plate 54) for the Church of the Ascension in Don Mills, Ontario. The theme was to be the church's namesake, the Ascension, a motif deriving from the biblical story of Christ's being taken up into the heavens after His resurrection. The window is appropriately exultant. It is designed with a nearly symmetrical composition that strongly suggests upward movement, and its colors are vivid.

In harmony with theological tradition, the Ascension is viewed as a cosmic event. "There's a cross at the top, broken up," Taylor points out. "I've used a mandala to link the bottom half of the window to the top. There is another mandala of sorts in the broken-up crown of thorns that runs up to either side of the cross. There are some landscape-type images, as well. The red is intended to be a force referring to the creation of the earth—massive upheavals, that sort of thing. Above that is water cooling it down. Below that is brown, for earth." Taylor agrees with many other artists that the cross is a difficult shape to integrate with other design elements; hence his decision to break up its pattern somewhat in order to merge it into the general scheme.

Perhaps because of its general shape, Taylor's window in the Church of the Messiah in Toronto (See Plate 55) is one of his most appealing works. Taylor was commissioned in 1979 to design and fabricate a new window for the eighty-seven-year-old Anglican church. A fire in the summer of 1976 had devastated the church's interior, and while the fire had left the walls standing, it had destroyed the east-by-southeast-facing chancel window. The interior had been carefully redesigned in order to preserve the spirit of the original architecture. The old window had had no particular theme, and the new one was to have a rather open-ended one: praise.

In England, Taylor had worked with John Hayward on a restoration in Blackburn Cathedral that incorporated glass from the cathedral's original windows. Taylor initially hoped to honor Messiah's old window by using its painted glass to provide more than half the materials used in the new one. Although it turned out that too much of the original glass had been severely damaged for it to be used to any great extent, Taylor was able to make use of some of the glass. A small example is found in some of the lettering at the window's bottom; but much of the old glass is too well integrated to pick out easily.

The result of nearly a year's efforts by Taylor and two assistants is a carefully designed, vigorously orchestrated stained-glass collage that unifies the window's fifteen individual panels. Taylor told us that he designed a window that was primarily abstract and that would invite the viewer to participate by projecting his or her own symbolic interpretations on its profusion of shapes. But the idea of praise seems wonderfully represented.

In his years since Wimbledon and the Royal College of Art, Taylor's stained-glass design work has nearly always had to conform to the specific requirements of particular situations. "When I was at college there were no limits to inventiveness," he comments. "These days, since I do architectural work, I have to come in from a particular direction. I like to think that each window has something to say. But the more commissions you do, the harder it is to stay fresh. Every five or six years I question the way I am going, completely." The variety of approaches taken in the windows we've chosen to present seem to offer evidence of Taylor's search for new directions.

Because he usually designs for churches, Taylor often draws on a range of Christian symbols, many of them from the vocabulary of the Gothic artists. He describes his usual procedure: "I set down the basics of a window and saddle bars [reinforcement bars] to scale. I then work out what symbols I wish to use. I will then start placing in the various symbols where I want them, moving them around, playing one shape against

PLATE 53: Chancel window, St. Mark's United Church, 1984. Diameter 6 ft. 10 in. (2.08 m diameter) Scarborough, Ontario.

J.R.

another. You get to a stage where you see a space where the most elegant leadline would be one flowing off at a curve from a particular place. There are some leadlines I will place in that are just a way of reducing the size of glass pieces and a way of backing up, or supporting, the design.

"Designing, for me, is extremely hard work," he adds. "Some days you're working on a design and it just isn't going anywhere. So you leave it for a while and come back to it, and you suddenly see the design freshly again. And you think, 'God, that's wrong.' And you erase the whole area and rework it or move it around."

Yet such revisions are actually alterations of a strong basic idea. "On reflection, I've found that the original idea I come up with for a job is the one I come back to," he says. "I may work my way through a thousand directions, but I come back to the first idea. By the time I've gone through the other directions, the first idea has matured, and it's involved some of the other directions."

Taylor regards the symbolic elements in his designs, including those from the Gothic repertoire, as "abstractions of natural symbols." Water, fire, the dove, the vine and grape cluster, the pomegranate, the brier of the crown of thorns — each of these is a natural thing or phenomenon, as well as a traditional Christian symbol. Taylor has lived in rural surroundings near Toronto for many of the years he has resided in Canada, and natural things are a part of his life. He studies what is around him, and his camera has become one of his design tools, for he relies upon it to capture forms that he may later use in designs.

But Taylor has other trusty design devices, as well. "If I'm stuck, design-wise, I usually pull the collage bag out. I dragged this garbage bag of bits and pieces, from all over Europe, with me to Canada," he declares with a grin. "It's got old bus tickets and all sorts of things in it, going back to the fifties. If there was a fire, it used to be the first thing I'd drag out of the house. When I'm really stuck, I use it. It's a way of blundering around in the dark. Piling stuff down onto a piece of card, you'll find a form, a shape, or whatever, within that mess." As haphazard as this particular stratagem may sound, Taylor thinks out the implications of everything he tries before the design is settled and construction begins.

With deep knowledge of the Western art tradition, a pragmatic familiarity with design processes, and a mastery of the nuts-and-bolts of stained-glass fabrication and installation, Stephen Taylor has a thorough understanding of his medium. During his years in Canada, he has endeavored to pass on various aspects of this understanding to others. Besides occasionally assuming the role of public lecturer and being the subject of articles and of interviews on radio and TV, Taylor has taught for extended periods at McMaster University and Humber College of Applied Arts and Technology. He has also had a number of apprentices and assistants at various times. With some notable exceptions, he feels that Canadians have not yet been willing to commit themselves to a truly earnest, passionate study of stained glass as an art form. He does not stoop to casting stones at hobbyists, whose creations he refers to with a forbearing smile as "macramé glass"; however, he scorns the lack of depth shown by many callow "glass artists" who have not had the art training to be confidently original with their designs. "The trouble is that few people assimilate their influences and go on. No one can design as well in the German style as Schaffrath or Schreiter. I don't know why they try. The originals are magnificent, but I don't know what this insistence on copying is. It's a dead end."

There can be no doubt that the example of such strong, original work as Taylor's, executed with such fine craftsmanship, will provide the kind of encouragement that the emerging Canadian stained-glass scene needs.

PLATE 54: (Overleaf, above) Church of the Ascension, 1982. 6 × 19 ft. (1.83 × 5.79 m) Don Mills, Ontario.

PLATE 55: (Below) Church of the Messiah, 1980. 14 × 17 ft. (4.27 × 5.18 m) Toronto, Ontario.

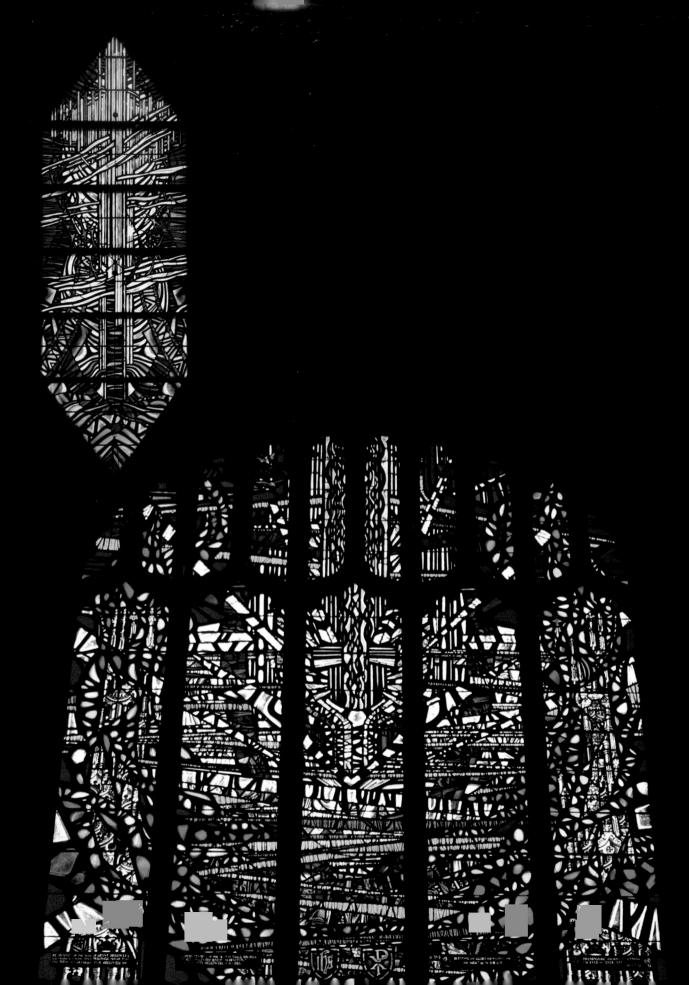

BIBLIOGRAPHY

Angus, Mark. *Modern Stained Glass in British Churches*. Oxford: A. R. Mowbray & Co., 1984.

Bartnev, Igor. *Modern Lithuanian Stained Glass*. Leningrad: Aurora Art Publishers, 1979.

Clarke, Brian. *Architectural Stained Glass*. New York and Toronto: McGraw-Hill, 1979.

Harrison, Martin. *Victorian Stained Glass*. London: Barrie & Jenkins, 1980.

Hill, Robert, et al. *Stained Glass: Music for the Eye*. Oakland, California: Scrimshaw Press, 1976.

Lee, Lawrence, et al. *Stained Glass*. New York: Crown, 1976.

McGrath, Raymond. *Glass in Architecture and Decoration*. London: Architectural Press, 1961.

Oidtmann, Friedrich, et al. *Licht Glas Farbe*. Aachen, Germany: M. Brimberg, 1982.

Pfaff, Konrad. *Ludwig Schaffrath: Stained Glass and Mosaic*. Krefeld, Germany: Scherpe Verlag, 1977.

Quagliata, Narcissus. *Stained Glass from Mind to Light*. San Francisco: Mattole, 1976.

Rigan, Otto. *New Glass*. San Francisco: San Francisco Book Co., 1976.

Sowers, Robert. *The Language of Stained Glass*. Forest Grove, Oregon: Timber Press, 1981.

PHOTO CREDITS

Appearing with each photograph of stained-glass art in this book are the initials of the photographer. Below is a list of the photographers with their names given in full.

PHOTOGRAPHERS

J.R.	Joel Russ	S.H.	Sarah Hall
D.W.	David Wilde	L.D.	Lauren Dale
R.J.	Robert Jekyll	B.L.	Barbara Laffey
F.D.	Fraser Day	B.H.	Peter ("Ben") Hogan
E.T.	Ernestine Tahedl	G.R.	Gundar Robez
P.D.	Peter Duthie	A.T.	Andrew Terris
L.H.	Lutz Haufschild	D.T.	Daniel Teichman

ACKNOWLEDGMENTS

Since we believed from the outset that this project was a collaborative venture, we would like to thank the following people for their help and encouragement along the way: Lutz Haufschild for his continued assistance throughout this project; all of the artists we interviewed, for their cooperation; Marianne Hodges for her assistance in translating; Bruno Freschi for providing the remarks on stained glass used on the jacket; and to the following people who provided accommodation and hospitality during our research trip: Bill and Ellen Schwartz, Jeff Trunkfield, Bev and Danny Ray, Neil Gallaiford and Gina Benvie, Mike Anstead and Lynn-Marie Holland, Rejene Stowe and Andrew Terris, David Wilde and Wendy Pope, and Rick Van Krugel. We also would like to gratefully acknowledge the support of the Canada Council.

192